DATE DUE	
APR 9 1984		
MAY 2 6 1988	AUG 0 4 2008	
AUG 1 1 1988	MAY 0 8 2009	
MAY 31 1990	AUG 10 2009	
FEB 0 2 1993	APR 2 8 2009	
DEC 2 7 1993	FEB 10 2010	
SEP 2 2 1997		
AUG 1 0 1996		

GYPSY

Random House
New York

Gypsy

A musical

*(Suggested by
the memoirs of
Gypsy Rose Lee)*

Book by
Arthur Laurents

Music by
Jule Styne

Lyrics by
Stephen Sondheim

To Erna Fillmore,
the grandest maternal cannibal of them all

GYPSY *was first presented by David Merrick and Leland Hay-
ward at The Broadway Theatre, New York City, May 21, 1959,
with the following cast:*

(IN ORDER OF APPEARANCE)

UNCLE JOCKO	Mort Marshall
GEORGE	Willy Sumner
ARNOLD (and his guitar)	Johnny Borden
BALLOON GIRL	Jody Lane
BABY LOUISE	Karen Moore
BABY JUNE	Jacqueline Mayro
ROSE	Ethel Merman
POP	Erv Harmon
NEWSBOYS	Bobby Brownell, Gene Castle, Steve Curry, Billy Harris
WEBER	Joe Silver
HERBIE	Jack Klugman
LOUISE	Sandra Church
JUNE	Lane Bradbury
TULSA	Paul Wallace
YONKERS	David Winters
L. A.	Michael Parks
ANGIE	Ian Tucker
KRINGELEIN	Loney Lewis
MR. GOLDSTONE	Mort Marshall
MISS CRATCHITT	Peg Murray
FARMBOYS	Marvin Arnold, Ricky Coll, Don Emmons, Michael Parks, Ian Tucker, Paul Wallace, David Winters

HOLLYWOOD BLONDES

AGNES	Marilyn Cooper
MARJORIE MAY	Patsy Bruder
DOLORES	Marilyn D'Honau
THELMA	Merle Letowt
EDNA	Joan Petlak
GAIL	Linda Donovan

Cow	Willy Sumner and George Zima
Pastey	Richard Porter
Tessie Tura	Maria Karnilova
Mazeppa	Faith Dane
Cigar	Loney Lewis
Electra	Chotzi Foley
Showgirls	Kathryn Albertson, Denise McLaglen, Barbara London, Theda Nelson, Carroll Jo Towers, Marie Wallace
Renée	Marsha Rivers
Phil	Joe Silver
Bougeron-Cochon	George Zima

Entire production directed and choreographed by
Jerome Robbins
Settings and lighting by Jo Mielziner
Costumes designed by Raoul Pène du Bois
Musical direction by Milton Rosenstock
Orchestrations by Sid Ramin *with* Robert Ginzler
Dance music arranged by John Kander
Additional dance music by Betty Walberg

The action of the play covers a period from the early twenties to the early thirties, and takes place in various cities throughout the country.

MUSICAL NUMBERS

Act One

1. "May We Entertain You"   BABY JUNE and BABY LOUISE
2. "Some People"   ROSE
3. Traveling
4. "Small World"   ROSE and HERBIE
5. Baby June and Her Newsboys
6. "Mr. Goldstone, I Love You"   ROSE and ENSEMBLE
7. "Little Lamb"   LOUISE
8. "You'll Never Get Away from Me"   ROSE and HERBIE
9. Dainty June and Her Farmboys
10. "If Momma Was Married"   LOUISE and JUNE
11. "All I Need Is the Girl"   TULSA and LOUISE
12. "Everything's Coming Up Roses"   ROSE

Act Two

1. "Madame Rose's Toreadorables"
         LOUISE and the HOLLYWOOD BLONDES
2. "Together, Wherever We Go"   ROSE, LOUISE and HERBIE
3. "You Gotta Get a Gimmick"   TESSIE, MAZEPPA and ELECTRA
4. "Small World"—Reprise   ROSE
5. "Let Me Entertain You"   LOUISE and COMPANY
6. "Rose's Turn"   ROSE

ACT ONE

Scene One

On either side of the proscenium, there are illuminated plac-ards—as in the days of vaudeville. After the overture, the placards light up to read:

UNCLE JOCKO'S KIDDIE SHOW
SEATTLE

The light illuminating the placards fades slowly as the curtain rises on the stage of a tacky vaudeville theatre.

*The stage is half-set for the rehearsal of a kiddie show. "*UNCLE JOCKO*"—the nervous, oily master of ceremonies—is surrounded by a pack of babbling kids and their tigress mothers. The kids are in horrible, homemade costumes; the mothers wear clothes of the very early twenties;* JOCKO *wears a tartan cap and fake horn-rimmed glasses as a concession to his name.*

JOCKO Everybody—SHUT UP! . . . All mothers—*out.* (*To his assistant*) Georgie, I don't want them in the wings, I don't want them in the theatre, I want them OUT!

GEORGIE It's a pleasure. O.K., mothers—this way. Move.
(*He herds them out as—*)

JOCKO All right, kids, get in a straight line along here and come forward one at a time. The doors open at seven and Uncle Jocko doesn't have enough time to rehearse your darlin' acts. (*He takes a simpering little girl completely covered with*

3

balloons out of line and moves her down, apart from the others) You wait here, girly-girl. (*Calling out front to the* SPOT MAN) Oh, Gus! Hit this doll with a surprise pink when she does her turn. (*To the girl*) Uncle Jocko promised the wee bairn would be a winner and she will. (*The kid kisses him coyly. To* GEORGIE) Chip off her sister's block. And you ought to see them balloons! O.K. Let's have the first wee laddie in Uncle Jocko's Kiddie Show. (*As a little boy with a big accordion comes forward,* JOCKO *speaks to the actual* CONDUCTOR *in the pit*) Take each of them from the top and then cut to the last eight. Every Friday night, ya ta ta, ya ta ta, Uncle Jocko dinna ken there were so many talented bairns right here in Seattle and the rest of the crap—ARNOLD AND HIS ACCORDION! (*As* ARNOLD *plays—indicating the kid*) Georgie, that's what's gonna kill vaudeville. All right, Arnold, cut to the end. The end, kiddo. (*He signals the* CONDUCTOR *for a sick chord;* GEORGIE *pushes* ARNOLD *off.* JOCKO *speaks to two little girls dressed as a Dutch boy and girl*) And who does Uncle Jocko have here? Who the hell does he—BABY JUNE AND COMPANY? . . . (*To the* CONDUCTOR) Half of the song, half of the dance, and off.

CONDUCTOR   Got ya.
      (*A small band starts the introduction*)

JUNE   (*Singing*)
   May we entertain you?
   May we see you smile?
   I will do some kicks—

LOUISE   (*Singing*)
   I will do some tricks.

4

ROSE (*From out front*)   Sing out, Louise—sing out!

JOCKO   Who said that?

JUNE (*Singing*)
I'll tell you a story.

LOUISE (*Singing*)
I'll dance when she's done.

ROSE (*From front*)   You're behind, Louise! Catch up, honey, catch up!

JOCKO   Who let in one of them mothers?

JUNE *and* LOUISE
By the time we're through entertaining you—
(*Coming down the aisle and onto the stage, carrying a little dog and a big handbag is—momma!*)

ROSE   Hold it, please, hold it! Save your strength, June. Louise, dear, if you don't count—

JOCKO   Madam, do you realize you are absolutely—

ROSE   I do, Uncle Jocko, but I want to save your very valuable time for you.

JOCKO   In that case—

ROSE   When I saw your sensitive face at the Odd Fellows Hall— my first husband was an Odd Fellow—

JOCKO   I am not an Odd Fellow!

ROSE   I meant a Knight of Pythias. My second husband was—

JOCKO   I'm not a Knight of Pythias!

ROSE   Then where *did* you catch our act?

JOCKO   At the Elks.

ROSE   My father is an Elk! I have his tooth here someplace. (*She dumps the dog into* JOCKO's *arms as she rummages in her handbag*) If you'll just hold Chowsie for me—that's short for chow mein. (*Baby talk*) Mommy just loves chow mein, doesn't she, Chowsie Wowsie? Stop sucking your thumb, Louise. (*To the* CONDUCTOR) Professor, I just marvel how you can make a performer into an artist.

JOCKO   (*Following her as she gads about*)   What is going on here??

ROSE   Now if you could help my little girls by giving them a good loud la da *da* de da da *da*—(*To* JOCKO, *whom she delicately shoves back as he moves to intervene*) God helps him who helps himself. (*To the* DRUMMER) Mr. Zipser—when the girls do their specialty would you please ad lick it? Show him, girls.

JOCKO   Is this really happening?!

ROSE   Oh, Gus? Gus, would you please slap Baby June with something pink? She's the star. Smile, Baby dear!

JOCKO   I have seen all kinds of mothers—

Mort Marshall, Ethel Merman, Karen Moore, and Jacqueline Mayro, as UNCLE JOCKO, ROSE, BABY LOUISE, and BABY JUNE

ROSE Do you know of a really good agent—don't hang on the baby, Louise, you're rumpling her dress—who could book a professional act like ours?

JOCKO A professional act! Hey, Georgie! Get a load of this crazy—

ROSE (*Suddenly grabbing him*) Don't you laugh! *Don't you dare laugh!* . . . That child is going to be a star.

JOCKO That's what they all say. All right—
     (*He shoves the dog back into her arms*)

ROSE But we're not finished!

JOCKO You are as far as I'm concerned.

ROSE Because you're trying to play favorites!

JOCKO (*Stops*) What?

ROSE How dare you let that rotten, untalented fat balloon block up my babies? I won't leave this stage till she does!

JOCKO That child—

ROSE Have you no loyalty to the Elks?

JOCKO I'm not an Elk!

ROSE Well, the editor of the *Gazette is!* I happen to know because at the last meeting he showed my father a letter he got—complaining some contest was fixed . . . I guess desperate people do desperate things. (JOCKO *stares at her, then motions the* BALLOON GIRL *to go.* ROSE *looks at the* CONDUCTOR, *and signals him as before*) La da *da* de da *da!* (*Music starts and the girls begin their act*) Thank you, Professor. Thank you, Uncle Jocko. (*She gives him the dog*) Thank you, Gus! Thank you, Mr. Zipser! Smile, girls, smile!

(*She is singing along with her girls when she sees the* BAL-LOON GIRL, *who has edged out from the wings. Still singing gaily,* ROSE *removes her hatpin. The* BALLOON GIRL *backs into the wings as* ROSE *marches after her, the hatpin extended like Joan of Arc's sword. Her dancing daughters watch, grin, and finish to a blare of music*)

The Lights Black Out

Scene Two

The illuminated placards change to read:

"HOME SWEET HOME"
SEATTLE

The scene is the kitchen of a frame house. Later that night.
We see an icebox, a sink overflowing with dishes; calendars and timetables on the walls, a rocker, etc.

LOUISE *and* JUNE *enter yawning, and take off the coats they wear over their costumes as* ROSE *slams in, throws her coat on a chair and heads for the icebox. She gives Chowsie, the little dog, to* LOUISE *as she gets a plate of food from the icebox. As usual, she is talking all the time.*

ROSE   That rotten little Uncle Jocko! He's as cheap as your grandpa. (*To* JUNE) Ten bucks for a talent like yours! Well, we're through with Kiddie Shows. *And* with your grandpa's lodge hall. It's time we moved on anyway! I'm gonna get us an agent to book the act on the Orpheum Circuit.

LOUISE   That's dog food, Momma.

ROSE   That's what she thinks. I'm hungry.

LOUISE   Then why didn't you eat some of our chow mein after the show?

ROSE   Because you two did the work and we gotta save every cent. (*To* JUNE, *who brings her a hair brush—as she brushes*

9

JUNE's *hair*) I had a dream last night: a whole new act for you!
Baby June and Her Newsboys!

LOUISE   Momma, do we have to stay in show business?

JUNE   Honest, Louise! How are you going to get the boys,
Momma?

ROSE   Louise can be a boy—(LOUISE *exits*)—and I'll find three
others.

JUNE   How are you going to pay them?

ROSE   The experience'll be their pay. I've got just enough saved
up for scenery and costumes. If I can squeeze a few bucks out
of Grandpa, we can head for Los Angeles and the Orpheum
Circuit. . . .
    (POP *enters. He is a crusty old man, holding the Bible he is
    eternally reading. A short pause*)

JUNE (*Tactfully*)   Good night, Momma. Good night, Grandpa.
    (*She exits*)

POP   You oughta be ashamed: fooling your kids with those
dreams!

ROSE   They're real dreams and I'm gonna make 'em *come* real
for my kids!

POP   What are you, Rose, a crazy woman?! God put you down
right here because He meant for you to stay right here!

ROSE   God's like me, Pop: we both need outside assistance.

POP You've squeezed the last penny outa me that you're ever gonna get!

ROSE It ain't for me! It's for my girls. It's too late for me.

POP It ain't too late for you to get a husband to support you.

ROSE After three husbands, I'm through with marriage. I want to enjoy myself. I want my girls to enjoy themselves and travel like Momma does!

POP And you'll leave them just like your mother left you!

ROSE Never! (*She turns to see* LOUISE, *who has entered behind her*) Why aren't you ready for bed, Louise?

LOUISE June says you said she can sleep with you tonight.

ROSE You know how high-strung the baby is after a performance.

LOUISE I performed.

ROSE It ain't the same. Now say good night and go to bed.

LOUISE Good night, Grandpa.
      (*She kisses him*)

POP Good night, Plug. You're a good girl.

ROSE You *are* a good girl and I was proud of you tonight.
      (LOUISE *runs to her and hugs her*)

LOUISE Momma, how come I have three fathers?

ROSE Because you're lucky. . . . You were born with a caul. That means you got powers to read palms and tell fortunes and wonderful things are going to happen for you!
(LOUISE *goes*)

POP Why do you fill her with such bunk?

ROSE It ain't bunk!

POP Nothin' wonderful is going to happen to her or June—or to you.

ROSE Maybe not to me, but they're gonna have a marvelous time! I'll be damned if I'm gonna let them sit away their lives like I did. And like you do—with only that calendar to tell you one day is different from the next! And that plaque—(*Pointing to a gold plaque on the wall*)—from your rotten railroad company to say congratulations: for fifty years, you did the same dull thing every dull day!

POP That plaque is a great tribute! It's solid gold!

ROSE How much could you get for it?

POP Rose, if you—

ROSE What good's it doin' sittin' there?!

POP That plaque belongs there like you belong home—instead of running around the country like a Gypsy!

12

ROSE   Anybody that stays home is dead! If I die, it won't be from sittin'! It'll be from fightin' to get up and get out! (*She sings*)

Some people can get a thrill
Knitting sweaters and sitting still—
    That's okay for some people who don't know they're alive;

Some people can thrive and bloom,
Living life in a living room—
    That's perfect for some people of one hundred and five!

But I
At least gotta try,
When I think of all the sights that I gotta see yet,
All the places I gotta play,
All the things that I gotta be yet—
    Come on, Poppa, whaddaya say?

Some people can be content
Playing bingo and paying rent—
    That's peachy for some people,
    For some humdrum people
To be,
But some people ain't me!

I had a dream,
A wonderful dream, Poppa,
    All about June and the Orpheum Circuit—
    Give me a chance and I know I can work it!
I had a dream,
Just as real as can be, Poppa—
There I was in Mr. Orpheum's office

And he was saying to me,
"Rose!
Get yourself some new orchestrations,
New routines and red velvet curtains,
Get a feathered hat for the Baby,
Photographs in front of the theatre,
Get an agent—and in jig time
You'll be being booked in the big time!"
Oh, what a dream,
A wonderful dream, Poppa,
And all that I need
Is eighty-eight bucks, Poppa!
That's what he said, Poppa,
Only eighty-eight bucks, Poppa . . .

POP   You ain't gettin' eight cents from me, Rose!
    (*He goes*)

ROSE (*Shouting after him*)   Then I'll get it someplace else—but
I'll get it and get my kids out! (ROSE *sings*)
Good-bye
To blueberry pie!
Good riddance to all the socials I had to go to,
All the lodges I had to play,
All the Shriners I said hello to—
Hey, L.A., I'm coming your way!
Some people sit on their butts,
Got the dream—yeah, but not the guts!
    That's living for some people,
    For some humdrum people,
I suppose.
    Well, they can stay and rot—

(*She starts out, comes back to take the plaque from the wall, dumps it in her purse, then finishes her song*)

But not
Rose!

(*And she strides out*)

The Lights Black Out

Scene Three

A road.

In front of the curtain, june *and* louise—*wearing their coats and hats and carrying suitcases—stand trying to thumb a ride. The music of "Some People" is continuous underneath. The cutout of a fancy old touring car "driven" by a rich man and his little son comes on and stops to pick up the children. But as they get in,* june *signals—and* rose *comes running out carrying a suitcase and Chowsie.*

She sings as the car "drives" across. Behind it, boys cross carrying signs indicating the lessening distance between Seattle and rose's *goal: Los Angeles.*

They pass an urchin tap dancing, his hat held out for money. rose *puts some pennies in his cap, then, impressed by his dancing, she yanks him into the car and they move on.*

A troop of boy scouts passes, singing. rose *hears the last little boy hold a good high note—and yanks him into the car.*

At last, they reach a welcome banner: los angeles. *The car stops.* rose *gets out with her daughters and the dog and the suitcases and the two stolen boys. The car drives away and as the little band marches off gaily,* rose *brings up the rear—with the rich man's tearful little boy, whom she has also stolen.*

The illuminated placards change to read:

"DON'T CALL US"
LOS ANGELES

The backstage of a vaudeville house. There are odds and ends of scenery, crates, trunks, lights, etc.

MR. WEBER, *the theatre manager, rushes on, followed by* ROSE *and her exhausted brood, who collapse near the wings.*

WEBER No, Madam Rose, no!

ROSE Now listen, Mr. Weber, I did not come all the way from Seattle to Los Angeles to take "No" for an answer.

WEBER You'll take it from me.

ROSE Because you don't know how to run your theatre. Your business is slipping. You need youth, fresh young talent.

WEBER Madam Rose, I told you this morning, I told you this afternoon and I am telling you now: if there is anything I hate worse than kids, it's kids on stage!

ROSE Children, go play in the alley. (*As they go*) Mr. Weber, that was a rotten remark. If you were a gentleman, you'd apologize and book my act.

WEBER   I am not a gentleman.
(*A nice-looking man carrying a suitcase enters. He has a sweetly sad, tired quality*)

ROSE   Oh, deep down, you are. And if you—

WEBER   (*To the man*)   Herbie! I been looking for you to get your opinion of the show.

HERBIE   I doubled your crackerjack order, Ed.

WEBER   That bad?

HERBIE   Except for a coupla acts. I left a memo on your desk.

ROSE   Mr. Weber, you left me right in the middle of a sentence.

WEBER   Madam Rose, you're always in the middle of a sentence.

ROSE   But if your show is as bad as this intelligent gentleman says, you could certainly try my act for a few nights. (*To* HERBIE) Couldn't he?

HERBIE   Yeah, he could. You could, Ed.

WEBER   What??

HERBIE   Your theatre gets a family audience. They love kids.

ROSE   And my kids are great!

HERBIE   They sure are.
(ROSE *and* WEBER *gape*)

WEBER How do you know?

HERBIE I've seen 'em.

WEBER Where?

HERBIE In—Seattle. They'd give your show a lift, Ed.

WEBER Well . . .

ROSE Listen—

WEBER Stop pushing. Let me think it over.
(*He goes*)

ROSE (*Pumps* HERBIE's *hand several times*) Gee—it's hard for me to say thanks!

HERBIE You just said it.

ROSE Why'd he listen to you?

HERBIE Everybody in show business listens to anybody. Besides, I used to book acts into this theatre.

ROSE Are you an agent?

HERBIE I was but I'm in the candy business now: I sell to vaudeville houses all over the West.

ROSE How could you ever leave show business?

HERBIE When the acts I handled had too little talent, I got sick to my stomach. Ulcers.

ROSE   You're too sympathetic.

HERBIE   Also I went bust. I was always giving them my commission and telling them they got a raise.

ROSE   The good Lord says charity begins at home.

HERBIE   I don't have a home.

ROSE (*Eyes him*)   You're not married?

HERBIE   I had five sisters, and the ugly one didn't get married until a year ago.

ROSE   . . . Why'd you help me just now?

HERBIE   I love kids.

ROSE   Oh.

HERBIE   Also—I saw you before.

ROSE   Where?

HERBIE   Waiting outside Weber's office. You looked like a pioneer woman without a frontier.

ROSE   I don't suppose you'd consider being an agent again.

HERBIE   Would you consider marrying again?

ROSE   How do you know I'm not married now?

HERBIE   I asked your kids about you.

ROSE   Oh. Well, after three husbands, it takes a lot of butter to get you back in the frying pan.

HERBIE   After twenty years of show business—(*Picks up bag*) —you kinda breathe better in the real world.

ROSE   Funny.
     (*Music starts*)

HERBIE   What?

ROSE   Us. I like you—but I don't want marriage. You like me— but you don't want show business.

HERBIE   That seems to leave you there—and me here.

ROSE   Oh, that depends on how you look at it. You look at what we don't have, I look at what we do have. (ROSE *sings*)
Funny, you're a stranger who's come here,
     Come from another town.
Funny, I'm a stranger myself here—
Small world, isn't it?
Funny, you're a man who goes traveling
     Rather than settling down.
Funny, 'cause I'd love to go traveling—
Small world, isn't it?

We have so much in common,
     It's a phenomenon.

We could pool our resources
By joining forces
   From now on.
Lucky, you're a man who likes children—
   That's an important sign.
Lucky, I'm a woman with children—
Small world, isn't it?
Funny, isn't it?
   Small, and funny, and fine.
      (*Music continues as* WEBER *returns*)

WEBER   Well, I'm not gonna pay you much money.

ROSE   Oh, you'll have to talk about money to Herbie.

WEBER   You handling her act?!

HERBIE   Well—no, I—(*Looks at her. She smiles in appeal and he laughs*)—yeah, I guess I am.

WEBER (*As he goes*)   I'll be in the office.

ROSE   (*Singing happily*)
We have so much in common,
   It's a phenomenon.
We could pool our resources
By joining forces
   From now on.

HERBIE   Rose . . . is that act of yours any good?

ROSE Good? It's great—and June is absolutely sensational!
Wait till you see it! (*Singing*)
Lucky, you're a man who likes children—
   That's an important sign.
Lucky, I'm a woman with children—
Small world, isn't it?
Funny, isn't it?
   Small, and funny, and fine.

The Lights Fade Out

Scene Five

The illuminated placards change to read:

BABY JUNE AND HER NEWSBOYS
LOS ANGELES

The curtains part to show a street drop typical of vaudeville; before it, a newspaper kiosk. The orchestra is a tacky, rickety vaudeville combination that tears into the screeching musical introduction for BABY JUNE AND HER NEWSBOYS. *The* BOYS, *of course, are* LOUISE *and the three little kids* ROSE *stole en route to L.A. Their costumes are cheap representations of newsboy outfits, and they wave papers wildly as they sing.*

NEWSBOYS (*Singing*)
Extra! Extra! Hey, look at the headline!
Historical news is being made!
Extra! Extra! They're drawing a red line
Around the biggest scoop of the decade!
A barrel of charm, a fabulous thrill!
The biggest little headline in vaud-e-ville:
(*Spoken—to ecstatic drum rolls*)
Presenting—in person—that three-foot-three bundle of dyna-mite: BABY JUNE!
(*There is the greatest drum roll of them all, and crashing through the "front page" plastered across the kiosk comes* JUNE, *wearing the gaudiest, fanciest, richest costume* ROSE *has been able to whip up. She whirls madly to the footlights, does a split and coyly screeches—*)

24

JUNE Hello, everybody! My name is June. What's yours?
(Then, assisted by the NEWSBOYS, JUNE *sings a ragtime version of "Let Me Entertain You")*

Let me entertain you,
Let me make you smile.
    Let me do a few tricks,
    Some old and then some new tricks—
I'm very versatile!
    And if you're real good,
    I'll make you feel good—
I want your spirits to climb.
So let me entertain you
And we'll have a real good time—yessir!
We'll have a real good time!

(After that, she tap dances wildly about the stage and does every trick ROSE *has been able to teach, steal and think up. She has a big finish—with the* BOYS *offstage, of course. She does high kicks for her bows and then, breathing as though each gasp were her last, she trips daintily to the footlights and says—)* Thank you so much, ladies and gentlemen. You're *very* kind . . . You know, everybody has someone to thank for their success. Usually, it's their mother; sometimes, it's their father. But tonight, I'd like you all to join me in giving thanks to an uncle of mine—and an uncle of yours. The Greatest Uncle of Them All: OUR—UNCLE—SAM! *(A crash from the orchestra and, as* JUNE *darts behind the kiosk to change her costume, the* NEWSBOYS *and* LOUISE *return—in military costumes. Each of the three* BOYS *represents a wing of our armed forces;* LOUISE *is Uncle Sam. Each child does whatever he can for a specialty;* LOUISE *does a trick step—which she also did in the opening. The* pièce de résistance *is, naturally,* JUNE. *This time she is dressed like a red,*

25

white, and blue Statue of Liberty and she is on point, twirling batons for all she is worth. Behind her, the American Eagle pops up over the kiosk; the band plays "The Stars and Stripes." But ROSE *takes no chances. As* JUNE *twirls herself into a split,* LOUISE *and the* BOYS *fire the rifles they are carrying—and American flags pop up. Wild applause, stopped by* JUNE, *breathing harder than ever)* Mr. Conductor, if you please.

(The orchestra strikes up again and JUNE *and her* NEWS-BOYS *start a traveling step. As the music builds and gets faster, the name of the city on the illuminated placard changes. It goes from one town to another, finally winding up with* AKRON. *During this, however, the lights on the performers begin to flicker faster and faster—and as* JUNE *and her* BOYS *seem to dance faster and faster, they appear to be flying through space and growing. Actually, through the flickering dissolve, they are replaced by another* JUNE, *another* LOUISE, *and other* BOYS—*all in the same costumes as the originals, but all older and bigger. Time has passed. The act is the same, but the cast is older and the placard has changed to read:*

DAINTY JUNE AND HER NEWSBOYS

AKRON

The music ends with a flourish. The older JUNE *blows the same coy kiss and does the same high-kick bow that the* BABY JUNE *did, and—thank heaven—)*

The Lights Black Out

SCENE SIX

The placards read:

"HAPPY BIRTHDAY"
AKRON

Two plaster-cracked hotel rooms.

An alarm clock is ringing wildly as the light comes up on the smaller room. It is festooned with clotheslines hung with winter underwear, costumes, etc. On the bare bedsprings of the one bed lies LOUISE, *wrapped up in a blanket of a very distinct pattern. The mattress has been put on the floor and on it, wrapped in another blanket of the same pattern, are three of the* BOYS *in the act. Asleep on two chairs pushed together is the oldest, best-looking and brightest boy in the act:* TULSA. *He is also wrapped in one of the blankets. There is one small window with the shade down.*

As the alarm keeps ringing, LOUISE *reaches out and shuts it off. A moment, then she bolts upright and looks around. Carefully then, she reaches out, sets the alarm off again and lies back quickly.*

YONKERS (*From the floor. A wiseguy*) Awright, awright!

L.A. (*Sweet-ass*) We're up, Madam Rose!

YONKERS (*Looks at clock*) Hey, it ain't even ten o'clock! Turn it off!

L.A. Louise!

27

TULSA (*Quietly*) Turn it off, Plug.

LOUISE (*Sits up and turns off the alarm. Yawns elaborately*) Was that the alarm?

YONKERS No, it was your mother singing! Shut up!

LOUISE I was having the loveliest dream. About a special day— My dream book says you dream about a day like that because it maybe really is your—

ANGIE We wanna sleep!

LOUISE I just wanted to say—(*She catches* TULSA's *eye. He shakes his head*) I'm sorry. (*Silence. She watches them return to sleep. Then she gets out of bed with a great clomping. No reaction. She goes to the window and considers the shade, finally yanking it up quickly. It rolls up with a tremendous clatter—but not a drop of light comes in: the window is smack up against a brick wall. She sticks her head out, craning her neck like mad to see the sky*) How can you all sleep on such a beautiful day!!

YONKERS Easy—if you shut up.

LOUISE Do you suppose that sun is so bright because—(JUNE *enters from the other room. Her hair is in curlers; she wears a frilly nightgown and robe*)

JUNE You woke up Mother.

LOUISE (*Whispering*) I didn't mean to, June. But today is
. . . well, you know.

JUNE Today is one day we don't have to travel and we don't
have to rehearse.

YONKERS Which means we could sleep!

LOUISE Is Momma mad?

JUNE She's in the bathroom—making coffee. (*To the* BOYS)
She says as long as *she's* up, everybody come have breakfast.

LOUISE June—

JUNE Honest, Louise!
(*She goes out as the* BOYS *groan.* LOUISE *groans back at
them*)

LOUISE I said I was sorry! (*A moment, then she timidly goes
into the other room. The light comes up just a trifle as she
enters, but the room is very dim. It is much larger than the
other room.* LOUISE *speaks, wistfully*) Momma? . . . Momma?

ROSE (*Calling*) Happy birthday! (*The bathroom door bursts
open and out comes* ROSE *in a battered bathrobe, carrying a
small birthday cake with lighted candles. She,* JUNE *and the*
BOYS—*who pop up and come crashing through the doorway—
sing "Happy Birthday" to* LOUISE, *who is startled and cries
happily. One of the boys turns on the lights and the room is
bright and gay. There is a big bed and a table near it. Little
dogs run about yapping; there are* JUNE's *cat, a monkey*

chained to the bed, and bird cages suspended from the chandelier, etc. There are yells of "Surprise! Surprise!" "Blow out the candles," "Make a wish," *hugs and kisses, etc.*) Make a wish!

LOUISE   I wish . . . oh, Momma, I wish—

ROSE   Oh! That rotten monkey ate a piece outa the cake! (*Going to the monkey*) Gigolo! Bad, Gigolo, bad bad! (*Then, looking at the blanket* LOUISE *has draped over her pajamas*) Say, that would make a good coat.
(LOUISE *blows out the candles*)

YONKERS   Hey, there's only ten candles on this cake!

ROSE   What do you care? You ain't gonna eat candles.

YONKERS   But she only had ten candles last year.

L.A.   And the year before that.

YONKERS   Come to think of it, she's had ten candles for the last—

ROSE   STOP RIGHT THERE! As long as we have this act, nobody is over twelve and you all know it! Excepting of course me and—where's Herbie? I had a dream— Tulsa, go across the hall and see what's keeping Herbie. The rest of you can give Louise her presents while I see if the chow mein is warmed up.

YONKERS   Chow mein?

LOUISE It's my birthday!

YONKERS But chow mein for breakfast??

ROSE Why not? There's egg roll, ain't there?
(*She exits into the bathroom*)

YONKERS If Madam Rose paid us a salary, we coulda *bought* you presents, Louise—(*He has picked up a box from under the bed*) But it's more fun to clip from the five and dime anyway. (*Hands her the box proudly*) It's a catcher's mitt and a big-league baseball.

LOUISE Thank you, Yonkers.

L.A. Here's a real stuffed cat.

ANGIE I clipped a bowl of goldfish. But they caught me, so I drew a fish instead.

LOUISE I love it. Oh, June, what a beautiful package!

JUNE It's a complete sewing set in a velvet-lined basket.
(*They embrace.* TULSA, *who has come back into the room, picks up his present—three second-hand books tied with cord—and puts it into* LOUISE's *hands*)

TULSA I should have wrapped them.

LOUISE (*Very touched*) You don't have to wrap books.

TULSA Well—happy birthday, Plug.

31

LOUISE Happy birthday, Tulsa. I mean, you're welcome.
(ROSE *comes out of the bathroom carrying food. During the following, the others help by arranging the plates and food*)

ROSE All right, one egg roll apiece and no more.

TULSA Herbie wasn't in his room, Madam Rose.

ROSE (*Stops dead*) . . . He wasn't?

TULSA No.

ROSE Where could he be?

LOUISE Momma, can I see my present from you, please?

ROSE It's from Herbie and me.

LOUISE It's not from Herbie. He's an agent. It's from *you*.

ROSE Well, I picked it out, but Herbie paid for it—with his commission for a whole month.

YONKERS Old Herb makes the same salary we do!

ROSE Inside, you, and get the coffee! (*Serving food*) Here I am, busting to tell Herbie the dream I had—

LOUISE Momma—

ROSE It's really in your honor, coming on the very evening of your birthday. (*To* JUNE) Oh, Baby! You'll love it. You all will. It's—(*Looks toward door, then makes a gesture of dismissal*)—children, it's a *new act!*

YONKERS   That ain't a dream, it's a miracle!

ROSE   In this dream, I saw June singing a song in like a barnyard. And then—a cow came on stage.

TULSA   A cow??

YONKERS   That's pretty sexy.

ROSE   Not a real cow. Sort of a dancing cow—with a great big smile. And that cow—that cow leaned right over my bed and spoke to me!

JUNE (*Fascinated*)   What did the cow say?
          (*A knocking on the door*)

KRINGELEIN (*Offstage*)   Madam Rose—

ROSE   I am *not* cooking in here, Mr. Kringelein. That cow—

KRINGELEIN   Open this door!

ROSE   I'm dressing. That cow—

KRINGELEIN   Madam Rose—

ROSE   I'll call you tomorrow when I'm finished. That dear fat cow looked me right in the eye and said: "Rose, if you want

33

to get on the Orpheum Circuit, put *me* in your act." Children, you know what I'm going to do?

YONKERS You're going to pay that crummy cow and not us!

ROSE I'm not paying anybody but I'm going to take that cow's advice! I'm going to call the new act: Dainty June and Her Farmboys. I'm going to get more boys. I'm going to put that cow in the act—(KRINGELEIN—*a pompous hotel manager— quietly opens the door of the other room, shuts it behind him and tiptoes to the doorway between the two rooms*)—and Chowsie and the monkey. And Louise's present—if you don't mind, honey—

LOUISE But, Momma, I don't even know what it is!

KRINGELEIN (*Coming into the room. Haughtily*) No cooking, Madam Rose?

ROSE How dare you enter a lady's boudoir without knocking?

KRINGELEIN (*Advancing*) Where's your hot plate?

ROSE Where's your search warrant?

KRINGELEIN (*Heading toward the bathroom*) In all the years I have been running a theatrical hotel—

ROSE (*Opening the corridor door*) If you don't leave, I'm going to scream!
        (*One of the boys darts to block the bathroom door*)

34

KRINGELEIN *(Pointing toward a sign)* You know the rules. No cooking. No electrical appliances. No—no pets other than small—*(Pushes the kid out of the way)*—dogs or—*(He opens the bathroom door. A little lamb in rubber drawers runs out between his legs and over to* LOUISE*)*

ROSE Happy birthday, darling!

KRINGELEIN It's a GODDAM ZOO!

ROSE Profanity in front of my babies! June, get the Bible! Get the Bible!
(People in bathrobes and wrappers begin to appear in the doorway, flowing into the room)

KRINGELEIN You pack up this dirty menagerie and get out!

ROSE You'll have to throw me out, you rotten ANIMAL HATER! *(To the others)* That's what he is! Send for the SPCA!

KRINGELEIN Send for the police! I rented these two rooms to one adult and three children! Now I see one adult! Five pets and one, two, three, four—

ROSE *(Points to one of the boys)* You counted him twice! *(The kids are running in and out. She turns to the others)* It's a simple little birthday party for my baby—

KRINGELEIN One, two, three, four—STAND STILL!

35

ROSE   Chow mein. I'd offer you some but there's only one egg roll—

KRINGELEIN   One, two, three, four, five—how many are sleeping in that room?

ROSE   What room?

KRINGELEIN   (*In the doorway between the two rooms*)   THIS room, madam, THIS room!

ROSE (*Pushing him in*)   There isn't a soul in this room.

KRINGELEIN   Now you know what I—

ROSE (*Closing the door behind them*)   Except you and me. (*She lets out a scream as she shoves him down onto the mattress on the floor*) Mr. Kringelein, what are you trying to do?!! (*Throws pillows and blankets on him*) Mr. Kringelein! Stop! Help! Help! (*She wrenches her robe open and staggers back into the other room, where the people get a chair for her and ad lib their concern as* ROSE *continues*) My babies! My babies! MONSTER! Thank you, Gladys. A little birthday party—chow mein—a tiny little cake—

(LOUISE, *with her lamb, goes into other room during this.* KRINGELEIN *gets out of the snarl of blankets and exits*)

HERBIE'S VOICE (*From the hall*)   Rose! Rose! Are you all right? (*He enters the room and pushes his way to* ROSE's *side*) Rose! What's happened? Are you O.K., honey?

ROSE (*Straightening herself*) Sure! Where have you—(*Then, remembering*) Herbie. Mr. Kringelein, the hotel manager, he—he tried to—to—

HERBIE (*A cynical eye*) Again?
(*He starts for the other room*)

ROSE Well, I had to do something, Herbie, don't you dare apologize to him!

HERBIE Where's Louise?

ROSE A fat lot you care. The child has a birthday—

HERBIE Does she like her present?

ROSE I'm surprised you remembered, where've you been? That's what I want to know.

HERBIE (*Bringing forward a mild little man*) Rose, this is Mr. Goldstone.

ROSE I ask you, Mr. Goldstone. The child has a birthday once a year. We plan a little party—I'm sorry it's such a small cake and—

HERBIE Mr. Goldstone is from the Orpheum Circuit.

ROSE There's only one egg roll and some fried . . . rice . . . and sub . . . gum . . . chow . . .

37

HERBIE   The act is booked on the Orpheum Circuit.

(*A long pause.* ROSE *stares, numb with a growing happiness. Mechanically, she picks up a plate from the trunk and holds it out*)

ROSE (*Singing*)

Have an egg roll, Mr. Goldstone,
Have a napkin, have a chopstick, have a chair!
Have a sparerib, Mr. Goldstone—
Any sparerib that I can spare, I'd be glad to share!
Have a dish, have a fork,
Have a fish, have a pork,
Put your feet up, feel at home.
Have a smoke, have a coke,
Would you like to hear a joke?
I'll have June recite a poem!
Have a lichee, Mr. Goldstone,
Tell me any little thing that I can do.
Ginger-peachy, Mr. Goldstone,
Have a kumquat—have two!
Everybody give a cheer—
Santa Claus is sittin' here—
Mr. Goldstone, I love you!
        (*Hysterical with excitement*)

Have a goldstone, Mr. Egg Roll,
Tell me any little thing that I can do.
Have some fried rice, Mr. Soy Sauce,
Have a cookie, have a few!
What's the matter, Mr. G.?
Have another pot of tea!
Mr. Goldstone, I love you!

There are good stones and bad stones
And curbstones and Gladstones
And touchstones and such stones as them!
There are big stones and small stones
And grindstones and gallstones,
But Goldstone is a gem.

There are milestones, there are millstones,
There's a cherry, there's a yellow, there's a blue!
But we don't want any old stone,
Only Goldstone will do!

ALL (*Singing*)
Moonstone, sunstone—we all scream for one stone!
Mervyn Goldstone, we love you!
Goldstone!
> (*The lights black out in the larger bedroom and fade in slowly on the small room, where a forgotten* LOUISE *sits with the lamb*)

LOUISE (*Singing softly*)
Little lamb, little lamb,
My birthday is here at last.
Little lamb, little lamb,
A birthday goes by so fast.
Little bear, little bear,
You sit on my right, right there.
Little hen, little hen,
What game shall we play, and when?
Little cat, little cat,
Ah, why do you look so blue?
Did somebody paint you like that,

Or is it your birthday, too?
Little fish, little fish,
Do you think I'll get my wish?
Little lamb, little lamb,
I wonder how old I am.
I wonder how old I am . . .

The Lights Dim Out

The placards change to read:

"TABLE FOR TWO"
NEW YORK

The scene is a section of a gaudy Chinese restaurant. HERBIE, *puffing away at a cigarette, sits at a table slightly detached from* ROSE *and* JUNE, *who are wearing coats made of the hotel blankets.* ROSE *is scraping leftovers from the plates into cartons which she eventually gathers into a paper sack. She hums happily.*

ROSE   Hand me June's plate, Louise.

JUNE (*Embarrassed*)   Mother—

ROSE   We're paying for it, ain't we? You'll get an ulcer like Herbie. Besides, what the dogs don't eat, we will.

HERBIE   Rose, did it ever occur to you there might be somebody in this world who *doesn't* like Chinese food?

ROSE   Don't be silly. Who? (*Hums, scrapes; then softly*) Don't you like it, Herbie?

HERBIE (*A beat, then he smiles*)   Sure, Rose. I love it.
        (LOUISE *enters wearing a blanket-coat and holding a little dog that is also wearing a blanket-coat*)

ROSE Did she?

LOUISE Yes.

ROSE (*Baby talk to the dog*) 'Atsa healthy-wealthy lady-wadie.

HERBIE Oh, God!

JUNE Herbie's angry: he's chain smoking.

ROSE Herbie's never angry; it's bad for his stomach. Come on, girls, beddie-bye.

JUNE It's so early!

ROSE You're going to audition for Mr. T. T. Grantziger and his Palace Theatre tomorrow and you have to look *young*.

LOUISE Can I wear a dress?

ROSE You'd look old in a dress. Besides, you haven't got one.

JUNE Good night, Uncle Herbie.
        (*She kisses him*)

HERBIE Good night, June. (*Stands up to kiss* LOUISE, *who stiff-arms him*) Good night, Louise.

LOUISE Good night, Herbie.
        (*She exits with* JUNE)

ROSE I'll cold-cream their faces and be right back.

HERBIE   The hotel is two doors away! Honestly, you behave as though those girls—Rose!
  (*This because she is collecting silverware and is about to put it in her bag*)

ROSE   We need new silverware. (*Stops, then puts down the silver. Quietly*) Herbie, how long is it going to take you to get used to me?

HERBIE   How long did it take me to get used to those coats?

ROSE   What's the matter with them? They're real stylish! Louise is very talented with a needle. Herbie, as the good Lord says: an eye for an eye, a tooth for a tooth—(*On this, she sweeps the silver into her bag*) And it serves them right for overcharging. (*Starts to go.* HERBIE *hands her a knife, which she also takes. But then she stops and returns*) They can skip the cold cream for one night. (*Automatically, he gets up and helps her off with her coat.* ROSE, *admiringly*) All this time we've been together, and you still stand up for me!

HERBIE   It's instead of standing up *to* you.

ROSE   O.K., you say we're never alone. I wanted to have dinner tonight, just the two of us, but what was I going to do with the girls? They're babies.

HERBIE   Rose, no matter how you dress 'em, no matter how you smother 'em, they're big girls. They're almost young women—

ROSE   They're not and they never will be!

HERBIE   I'm embarrassed in front of them! When are you going to marry me, Rose?

ROSE   Don't forget to take our scrapbooks to Mr. Grantziger's tomorrow.

HERBIE   When are you going to quit stalling?

ROSE   We got to show him proof that we headlined on the Orpheum.

HERBIE   Rose—

ROSE   All right: so it was a long time ago.

HERBIE   (*Gets up*)   Rose, if I walk out, you'll be stuck with the check! (ROSE *pulls* HERBIE *back into the chair*) Honey, don't you know there's a depression?

ROSE   Of course I know! I read *Variety*.

HERBIE   Don't you know what it's doing to vaudeville? Don't you know what the talkies are doing to vaudeville? Don't you know I love you?

ROSE   You think I'd be unfaithful to my husbands if you didn't? But I have to think of my girls and their happiness.

HERBIE   Louise is very happy being the front end of a cow!

ROSE   It's better than being the rear end! Anyway, she loves animals.

44

HERBIE   She and June should both be in school—

ROSE   And be just like other girls; cook and clean and sit and die! (*To a passing waitress, sweetly*) Honey, could I have a spoon to stir my tea? . . . Herbie, I promised June I'd make her a star and I will. I promised I'd get her on the Pantages Circuit and I did. I promised I'd get her on the Orpheum Circuit and I did.

HERBIE   *I* did! And you promised me that after I did, you'd marry me.

ROSE   I promised her she'd headline on Broadway and—

HERBIE   Didn't you hear what I said?

ROSE   Yes, but I'm ignoring it. (*To the waitress, for the spoon*) Thanks, honey. Herbie, it isn't very polite for a gentleman to remind a lady that she welched. There was no date on that promise—

HERBIE   ROSE, STOP HANDING ME—

ROSE   Your stomach! (*Quickly handing him a pill*) Herbie, why don't you get angry outside, instead of letting it settle in your stomach?

HERBIE   I'm afraid.

ROSE   Of me?

HERBIE   Of me.

ROSE   What do you mean?

HERBIE   If I ever let loose, it'll end with me picking up and walking.

ROSE   Only around the block.

HERBIE   No.

ROSE   Don't say that. (*Sings*)
   You'll never get away from me.
   You can climb the tallest tree,
      I'll be there somehow.
   True, you could say, "Hey, here's your hat,"
   But a little thing like that
      Couldn't stop me now.
   I couldn't get away from you
   Even if you told me to,
      So go on and try!
   Just try,
   And you're gonna see
   How you're gonna not at all get away from me!

HERBIE   What is it? What do you want? There are better agents.

ROSE   Not for me.

HERBIE   And even weaker men.

ROSE   Not for me.

HERBIE   Then what?

46

ROSE   You. Oh, Herbie, just help me like you been helping. Just let me get June's name up in lights so big, they'll last my whole life.

HERBIE   Rose, what you expect—

ROSE   I'll *get!* And after I get it, I promise I'll marry you. (HERBIE *moves away from the table*) I even promise to keep my promise. (*Silence*) Please, Herbie. I don't want to upset anything before the audition tomorrow. Including your stomach.

HERBIE (*Singing*)
Rose, I love you,
But don't count your chickens.

ROSE (*Singing*)
Come dance with me.

HERBIE
I warn you
That I'm no Boy Scout.

ROSE
Relax a while—come dance with me.

HERBIE
So don't think
That I'm easy pickin's—

ROSE
The music's so nice—

HERBIE

> Rose!
> 'Cause I just may
> Some day
> Pick up and pack out.

ROSE

> Oh no, you won't,
> No, not a chance.
> No arguments,
> Shut up and dance.

> You'll never get away from me,
> You can climb the tallest tree—
> I'll be there somehow!

> True, you could say "Hey, here's your hat,"
> But a little thing like that
> Couldn't stop me now.

BOTH

> I couldn't get away from you
> Even if I wanted to—

ROSE

> Well, go on and try!
> Just try—

HERBIE

> Ah, Rose—

ROSE

> And you're gonna see—

48

HERBIE

Ah, Rose—

ROSE

How you're gonna not at all
Get away from me!

The Lights Fade

Scene Eight

The placards change to read:

GRANTZIGER'S PALACE

NEW YORK

The scene is the stage of a good theatre.
*A telephone is ringing as the lights come up on the gold theatre curtains. An attractive, smartly groomed secretary—*CRATCHITT—*hurries on, signals toward the top of the theatre, pulls out a telephone attached on a bracket to the proscenium and answers.*

CRATCHITT Yes, Mr. Grantziger . . . I know, but they're having a little difficulty with their scenery. Well, wait till you see it . . . I am trying, Mr. Grantziger.
(Rose appears wearing a hat and coat)

ROSE *(To the* CONDUCTOR*)* Now keep the tempo bright. Keep it up.

CRATCHITT *(On phone)* That's the mother . . . I *have* told her!

ROSE *(Peering out front)* Hello, Mr. Grantziger. Where is he?

CRATCHITT *(Pointing)* In his office at the top of the theatre.

ROSE *(Waving—neighborly)* Hi!

50

HERBIE (*Runs on to try to get* ROSE *off*)   It's a privilege to audition for you, Mr. Grantziger!

ROSE (*Just before* HERBIE *drags her off*)   You're going to love us!
(*They exit*)

CRATCHITT (*Into the phone*)   That's the agent. *He's* nice.

HERBIE (*Returning*)   We're ready now.

CRATCHITT (*Into the phone*)   They're ready now, Mr. Grantziger. (*To* HERBIE) Good luck.

HERBIE   Thank you.
(*They both go off, the lights dim and the curtains part to reveal a corny set of a vaudeville barnyard, complete with haystack.* ROSE'S NEWSBOYS *are now* FARMBOYS, *and they stand with rakes, hoes, etc., in a picturesque tableau (!) as birds and music twitter the approach of dawn—which comes up violently. The music crashes into the introduction for the* NEWSBOYS' *song—sung, this time, by the* FARMBOYS—*and on cue, the haystack parts for* DAINTY JUNE *to whirl out and down front, where she ends in that same split. This time, she sings and dances with a cow, however. During the dance, the front end of the* COW *does a familiar trick step:* LOUISE *is still doing her big specialty*)

FARMBOYS (*Singing*)
Extra! Extra! Hey look at the headline!
Historical news is being made!
Extra! Extra! They're drawing a red line

Around the biggest scoop of the decade!
A barrel of charm, a fabulous thrill!
The biggest little headline in vaud-e-ville!
  (*Spoken*)
Presenting—in person—that five-foot-two bundle of dyna-
mite: DAINTY JUNE!

JUNE Hello, everybody! My name is June. What's yours? (*She
sings*)
I have a moo cow, a new cow, a true cow
Named Caroline.

COW Moo moo moo moo—

JUNE
She's an extra special friend of mine.

COW Moo moo moo moo—

JUNE
I like everything about her fine.

COW Moo moo moo moo—

JUNE
She likes to moo in the moonlight
  When the moody moon appears.
And when she moos in the moonlight,
  Gosh, it's moosic to my ears!
  She's so moosical . . .
She loves a man cow, a tan cow who can cow
  Her with a glance.
    (*The* cow *recites, "Moo moo moo moo," following this
    and the next two lines*)

When he winks at her, she starts to dance,
It's what grownups call a real romance,
But if we moved to the city
    Or we settled by the shore,
She'd make the mooooooooove,
    'Cause she loves me more!
        (JUNE *and the* COW *continue the dance to the end and exit.*
        The phone rings. CRATCHITT *comes on to answer*)

CRATCHITT (*Into the phone*)   Yes, Mr. Grantziger. Dainty June,
will you come out please? (JUNE *comes on*) Face front, dear.
Profile. (ROSE *appears in the other wing*) Yes, Mr. Grantziger.
Thank you. That's all.

ROSE   But we have a great dramatic finale!

CRATCHITT   I'm sure. But he's seen quite enough.

ROSE (*To the* CONDUCTOR)   Hit it!

CRATCHITT   But Mr. Grantziger does not want to see any—
        (*But even while she is talking, the music crashes in and*
        the FARMBOYS—*directed by* ROSE—*dance on in Eton suits*
        with high hats and canes, frightening CRATCHITT *off. They*
        launch into the song and tap dance that always built up to
        the entrance of the blond star. And it does this time, for
        JUNE *comes on, dazzling, glamorous, singing and dancing*
        for all she—and ROSE—*are worth. During the* BOYS' *num-*
        ber, one of the high hats falls off, and ROSE *dashes out from*
        the wings to retrieve and replace it. At the end of JUNE'S
        song-and-dance with the BOYS, ROSE *helps the stagehands*

get the haystack offstage. Behind it is the front of a train which puffs smoke)

FARMBOYS (*Singing*)
Broadway, Broadway! We've missed it so!
We're going soon and taking June
To star her in a show!
Bright lights! White lights!
Rhythm and romance!
The train is late so while we wait
We're gonna do a little dance!
    (*And they do—as a prelude to* JUNE's *song*)

JUNE (*Singing*)
Broadway! Broadway! How great you are!
I'll leave the farm with all its charm
To be a Broadway star!
Bright lights! White lights!
Where the neons glow!
My bag is packed, I've got my act.
So all aboard, come on, let's go!

YONKERS (*Calls*)   All aboard!

ROSE   Woo woo . . . Watch this! It's a train.

FARMBOYS   Let's go!
    (*Waving and "good-byes" from everybody. A train effect; the* COW *tries to run after the train*)

JUNE (*To the* COW)   Good-bye, Caroline. I'll write to you.

COW Moo!

JUNE Good-bye, Caroline—take care. Don't forget to write! . . . Wait! Stop the train! (*A chord*) Stop everything! I can't go to Broadway with you!

TULSA Why not, Dainty June?

JUNE (*To soupy music*) Because everything in life that really matters is right here! What care I for tinsel and glamour when I have friendship and true love? I'm staying here with Caroline!

>   (*She runs off the train platform and embraces the* COW *to general cheering. A chord from the orchestra—which launches once again into "The Stars and Stripes"; this time the American Eagle—and a big one—pops up over the train;* JUNE *grabs batons from the platform and twirls them madly as she marches downstage to end in a triumphant split while the* FARMBOYS *fire American flags from their canes.* ROSE *has done it again. The gold curtain closes on this heart-rending sight and the phone is ringing loudly.* CRATCHITT *comes out to answer it.* ROSE *and* HERBIE *come out from the opposite wing to hear the verdict*)

CRATCHITT Yes, Mr. Grantziger . . . What?? (*To* ROSE *and* HERBIE, *in astonishment*) He liked it! (*On the phone again*) Yes, sir. Yes, sir, if that's want you want. (*Hangs up and turns to* ROSE) If you and your tribe will come up to the office—I'll make out the contracts.

>   (*She shoots a peculiar look up to Mr. Grantziger's office and exits as* ROSE *shouts up*)

55

ROSE You won't be sorry, Mr. Grantziger! (HERBIE *yanks her off, but she is right back to add*) This is gonna make ya!

The Lights Black Out

Scene Nine

An ornately Gothic office with two doors. JUNE *is playing the piano madly while* LOUISE *hurls herself around the room in an improvised "interpretive" dance, possibly explaining it to* JUNE *in a phrase or two. The ringing of the telephone does not stop them. Then through one of the doors comes* CRATCHITT. *The girls stop their artistic efforts, embarrassed, but the piano keeps playing: it is electric.* CRATCHITT *turns it off and answers the phone.*

CRATCHITT Yes? . . . No. Mr. Grantziger's busy. He's gone down to the stage. (*Hangs up*) Your mother and her friend are just reading over the contract. They won't be much longer. She's gotta eat *some*time . . . Say, woman to woman, how old are you?

JUNE Nine.

CRATCHITT Nine *what?*

JUNE Nine going on ten.

CRATCHITT How long has that been going on?
    (HERBIE *comes in carrying a contract, followed by* ROSE)

HERBIE Miss Cratchitt, I think Mr. Grantziger made a mistake in this contract.

CRATCHITT (*Gaily*) So do I. (*The phone rings.* CRATCHITT *picks it up*) Yes?

ROSE You happy, girls?

LOUISE Yes, Momma.

CRATCHITT No.
(*She hangs up*)

HERBIE Miss Cratchitt, we were auditioning for Grantziger's Palace. This contract is for Grantziger's Variety.

CRATCHITT That's right.

HERBIE But the Variety is way down on Twelfth Street.

CRATCHITT He'll give you a visa to get there. (*The phone rings again*) Yes?

HERBIE I'd like to talk to Mr. Grantziger.

CRATCHITT (*Hangs up quickly*) No. Listen, I told you: he's down on the stage.

HERBIE (*Going toward the second door*) This the way?

CRATCHITT You can't disturb him. He's still holding auditions.

HERBIE Then I'll wait.

CRATCHITT Look, friend. Strictly between us, if I were you I'd sign that contract. There's only one item in that act of yours that the Boss likes: Dainty Little June. He thinks she can be an actress.

58

ROSE (*As* JUNE *stands up*)   He's right.

CRATCHITT   Can be—*if*.

HERBIE   If what?

CRATCHITT   If she goes to school for a solid year and takes lessons. He's ready to pay for everything—on one condition. (*To* ROSE) You stay away.

ROSE   Stay away? I'm her mother!

CRATCHITT   You said it, I didn't.

HERBIE   What about the act?

CRATCHITT (*Shrugs*)   One week at the Variety.

ROSE   But June *is* the act! How is it supposed to go on without her?

HERBIE   Rose, we could—

ROSE (*To* CRATCHITT)   How are Louise and I supposed to live?

CRATCHITT   You might get a job, dear.

ROSE   I have a job, dear, and I do it damn well! My daughters are my job and I have two of them!

LOUISE   Momma, if June—

ROSE June is my baby! I'm her mother!
(*The phone rings*)

CRATCHITT (*Answering*) Yes—

ROSE (*Taking it away and putting the receiver down on the table*) Don't you dare answer the phone when I'm yelling at you! Nobody knows June like I do and nobody can do for her what I can!

JUNE Momma, this is my chance to be an actress. Mr. Grantziger can make me a star!

ROSE You *are* a star! And I made you one! Who's got clippings like she has? Look at 'em! Books full of 'em! She don't need lessons any more than she needs Mr. T. T. Grantziger!

CRATCHITT There isn't a person in show business who doesn't need Mr. Grantziger!

ROSE Take a good look at *this* person!

HERBIE Rose—

ROSE They're so smart in New York!

CRATCHITT New York is the center of everything.

ROSE New York is the center of New York! There's a whole country full of people who *know* people!—who know what a mother means to her daughter! It's hicks like you who don't

know! And you want to know something else? Grantziger's a
hick! He'll get no place!

HERBIE   Rose—

ROSE   He's trying to take my baby away from me, that's what
he's trying to do! Well, over my dead body, he will!
   (*And she storms out the door to the "stage," with* HERBIE
   and CRATCHITT *calling and running out after her. A pause,
   then* LOUISE *picks up the phone left off the hook*)

LOUISE   (*Quietly*)   No. (*Hangs up*) Momma's just talking big,
June. She won't really—

JUNE   Yes, she will.

LOUISE   Maybe Mr. Grantziger will—

JUNE   No, he won't . . . Well, that's show business.

LOUISE   Aren't you happy someone like Mr. T. T. Grantziger
thinks you can be a star?

JUNE   You're funny.

LOUISE   Why?

JUNE   You're never jealous.

LOUISE   Oh. Well, I don't have any talent. I don't really mind—
except Momma would like it better if I did.

JUNE   I guess that's what she likes about me. Momma's no fool. I'm not a star.

LOUISE   You are.

JUNE   *I'm not!* Mr. Grantziger could make me one if she only didn't—
     (*Her voice cracks.* LOUISE *puts an arm around her*)

LOUISE   Momma can make you a star, too.

JUNE   (*In control again, moves away*)   Momma can do one thing: she can make herself believe anything she makes up. Like with that rhinestone finale dress *you* sewed for me. Momma wants publicity so she makes up a story that three nuns went blind sewing it! Now she believes it. She even believes the act is good.

LOUISE   Isn't it?

JUNE   (*Cold anger*)   It's a terrible act and I hate it! I've hated it from the beginning and I hate it more now! I hate pretending I'm two years old. I hate singing those same awful songs, doing those same awful dances, wearing those same awful costumes —I didn't mean it about the costumes.

LOUISE   No. You just meant you're too big for them now.

JUNE   Do you ever feel like you didn't have a sister?

LOUISE   . . . Sometimes.

62

JUNE It's Momma's fault.

LOUISE You can't blame everything on Momma.

JUNE *You* can't maybe. I wish she'd marry Herbie and let me alone.

LOUISE Herbie doesn't want to marry her. All he cares about is the act.

JUNE Honest, Louise.

LOUISE Well, he's an agent!

HERBIE (*Enters and tosses the contract back on the desk*) Your mother isn't feeling well. I'm going to take her back to the hotel . . . Don't worry, I'll get you a good booking.
(*He exits*)

LOUISE I wish Momma would marry a plain man . . . so we'd all be together. (*She sings*)
If Momma was married we'd live in a house,
As private as private can be:
Just Momma, three ducks, five canaries, a mouse,
Two monkeys, one father, six turtles and me . . .
If Momma was married.

JUNE (*Singing*)
If Momma was married, I'd jump in the air
And give all my toeshoes to you.
I'd get all these hair ribbons out of my hair,
And once and for all, I'd get Momma out, too . . .
If Momma was married.

LOUISE

Momma, get out your white dress!
You've done it before—

JUNE

Without much success—

BOTH

Momma, God speed and God bless,
We're not keeping score—
What's one more or less?
Oh, Momma, say yes
And waltz down the aisle while you may.

LOUISE

I'll gladly support you,
I'll even escort you—

JUNE

And I'll gladly give you away!

BOTH

Oh, Momma, get married today!

JUNE

If Momma was married there wouldn't be any more—
"Let me entertain you,
Let me make you smile.
I will do some kicks."

LOUISE

"I will do some tricks."

JUNE
Sing out, Louise!

LOUISE
Smile, baby!
Momma, please take our advice:
We aren't the Lunts.

JUNE
I'm not Fanny Brice.
Momma, we'll buy you the rice,
If only this once

BOTH
You wouldn't think twice!
It could be so nice
If Momma got married to stay.

LOUISE
But Momma gets married—

JUNE
And—

LOUISE
Married—

JUNE
And—

LOUISE
Married

BOTH

And never gets carried away.
Oh, Momma,
Oh, Momma,
Oh, Momma, get married today!

The Lights Dim Out

The placards change to read:

"DREAMS OF GLORY"
BUFFALO

A theatre alley, with steps that lead up to the stage door.
Without music, TULSA is dancing, rehearsing a routine with a broom for a partner. HERBIE comes out the stage door and watches until TULSA sees him and stops in embarrassment.

HERBIE That's pretty fancy footwork, Tulsa. Why don't you show it to Madam Rose?

TULSA I'm not that good, Herbie. It's just foolin' around.

HERBIE (*As, unseen by him, LOUISE enters*) You started "foolin' around" about three months ago. Just after Mr. Grantziger canceled our booking.

TULSA Well . . .

HERBIE Why, Tulsa?

LOUISE He's just had more time, that's all. Like that two-week layoff in Albany.

TULSA And the layoff in Rochester.

LOUISE And the layoff in Niagara Falls.

HERBIE   Oh. I thought you were maybe worried about the act.

TULSA   Oh, no, Herbie.

HERBIE   Because the way things are pickin' up—why, I wouldn't be surprised if you kids got paid! (*To* LOUISE) Matter of fact, they're good enough right now for me to treat you to an ice-cream soda.

LOUISE   No, thank you.

HERBIE   Chow mein?

LOUISE   Momma doesn't like us to eat just before a show.

HERBIE   (*After a moment, gently*)   Louise—there's one thing your momma knows that I wish you did: I like her.
        (*He starts toward the stage door*)

LOUISE   Herbie . . . (*He stops. A moment, then she shakes her head*) Nothing.

HERBIE   Tulsa, if you or any of the boys have any problems, you bring 'em to me.

TULSA   Sure, Herbie.
        (HERBIE *exits*)

LOUISE   You didn't tell him, did you? I mean that you're re-hearsing a dance-team act?

TULSA   How'd you know I was?

LOUISE I saw you practicing Monday after the matinée, with your broom for a partner. I was up in the flies.

TULSA Louise—

LOUISE Oh, I won't tell anybody, Tulsa! I'm very secretive. Just like you. (*Takes his hand*) See? That's what this means in your palm. And this means you make up dreams—just like me.

TULSA (*Moves away*) What do you make up dreams about, Louise?

LOUISE . . . People.

TULSA Oh, I do that too.

LOUISE Yes, but yours are about a partner for your act.

TULSA She's gonna be more than a partner, I hope. I mean I dream . . . well, you know . . .
(*He starts to dance around*)

LOUISE What would she have to be like, Tulsa? A wonderful singer and dancer, I guess.

TULSA No. I'm going to do most of that. I don't mean I'm going to hog it but—they always look at the girl . . . in a dance team. Especially if she's pretty.

LOUISE Makeup can help. And costumes.

TULSA I've got the costumes all figured out. A blue satin tux for me—

69

LOUISE   With rhinestone lapels—

TULSA   You think?

LOUISE   I'll sew them on.
        (*Music*)

TULSA (*As the music starts*)   O.K. Thanks. Well, I pretend I'm
   home getting ready for a date. I'm combing my hair. I take a
   flower. Put it in my lapel. Then I spot the audience. (*He sings*)
Once my clothes were shabby,
Tailors called me "Cabbie,"
So I took a vow,
   Said "This bum'll
   Be Beau Brummel."
Now I'm smooth and snappy,
Now my tailor's happy.
   I'm the cat's meow,
   My wardrobe is a wow:
Paris silk, Harris tweed,
There's only one thing I need.
Got my tweed pressed,
Got my best vest,
   All I need now is the girl!
Got my striped tie,
Got my hopes high,
   Got the time and the place, and I got rhythm—
   Now all I need's the girl to go with 'em!
If she'll
Just appear, we'll
   Take this big town for a whirl,

And if she'll say, "My
Darling, I'm yours," I'll throw away my
Striped tie and my best-pressed tweed—
All I really need
Is the girl!

(LOUISE *has been watching with yearning and now, as*
TULSA *begins to dance, the yearning increases. He explains*
his dance to her as he goes along)

I start easy . . . Now I'm more—debonair . . . Break! And I
sell it here . . . I start this step—double it—and she appears!
All in white! (*He reaches out his hand to the invisible partner,*
and LOUISE—*who has gotten up—holds out her hand, tenta-*
tively. He is unaware of her, unaware of her hopes, unaware
she is following him about, visualizing herself as the partner
for him) I take her hand—kiss it—and lead her out on the floor
. . . This step is good for the costumes . . . Now we waltz.
Strings come in. And I lift her! . . . Again! . . . Once more!
. . . Now the tempo changes; all the lights come up; and I
build for the finale! (*At last, he starts a step that* LOUISE *knows,*
and, clumsily, she starts to do it with him. At last, he notices
and shouts) That's it, Louise! But do it over here! Give me
your hand! Faster! Now Charleston right! Again! Again!
Turn!

(*She is dancing joyously, her happiness making up for her*
awkwardness. They end together—in triumph. L.A. *runs*
in from the stage door in costume for the Cow Act and
whistles to them. They get up and race into the theatre)

The Lights Dim Out

The placards change to read:

"TERMINAL"
OMAHA

*The scene is a railroad platform. It is a misty night. Baggage is
piled near* ROSE *and* HERBIE. YONKERS *and* ANGIE *are there.*

ROSE Don't lower yourself to argue, Herbie. If those rats want
to quit the act, let them quit. If they want their train tickets
home, give them their bus tickets home. (*Crossing*) What's
keeping those girls?

HERBIE There's plenty of time, Rose.

ROSE (*Going to the end of the platform, peering out*) And you
say they're big enough to take care of themselves.

HERBIE Look, fellas, I know we've had a couple of layoffs in
the—

YONKERS It ain't that, Herbie.

HERBIE Then what is it?

YONKERS We're—too old.

HERBIE (*Sotto voce*) Would you be too old if Madam Rose and
I could see our way clear to increasing your salary?

72

ROSE (*A bellow from clear across the stage*)   Increase what salary?!

ANGIE   Herbie's been paying us—

YONKERS (*Kicks him*)   Moron!

ROSE (*Coming back*)   Herbie . . .

HERBIE   How long is it going to take you to get used to me, Rose?

ROSE (*Gently*)   Button your coat. (*To the* BOYS) Ingrates! You take the bread out of that man's mouth and spit it in his face! Well, as the good Lord says, "Good riddance to bad rubbish." Give 'em their tickets, Herbie. They were both rotten in the act anyway.

HERBIE   O.K.
  (*He takes out tickets as she peers out for the girls*)

YONKERS   Thanks, Herbie. Only we'd like tickets for all the fellows.

HERBIE   . . . All the fellows?

YONKERS   Well, they asked us.

HERBIE   You're all leaving?

ANGIE   Yes, sir, Herbie.

ROSE   Something's funny. Something's very funny here.

HERBIE   Why, Angie?
  (*Silence*)

ROSE   What's this all about?
  (*Silence*)

HERBIE   O.K. If you're all going, you're all going. But why, Yonkers—
  (LOUISE *runs on, a note in her hand*)

ROSE   Where've you been? Where's June? (*Silence*) Louise, where's June? (LOUISE *holds out the note*) Don't give me any of your poems to read now. Answer me!

LOUISE   June wrote this. To you.

ROSE   Wrote what? What's she writing me for?

LOUISE   Momma, *read it!*
  (ROSE *looks at her, then takes the letter. She reads it, then sits and stares at it, not moving, looking like a dead woman through the following*)

ANGIE (*To* HERBIE)   She eloped.

YONKERS   She didn't elope, stupid. They got married three weeks ago.

HERBIE   Who got married?

YONKERS   June and Tulsa. Only they hadda wait till their act was ready before they took off.

74

ANGIE It's a keen act. Ain't it, Louise?

LOUISE I didn't see it.

YONKERS We ain't rats, Herbie. We just knew that without June—

HERBIE Where'd they go?

ANGIE Well, first they got a club date in Kansas City . . .

YONKERS (*Kicks him*) Big mouth! Could we have the tickets now, please, Herbie? We gotta get moving. See, we fixed up an act of our own and—

HERBIE (*Suddenly, looking at* ROSE) Get moving!

L.A. Don't be sore, Herbie. Geez, it ain't our fault the act's washed up.
(*He and* ANGIE *start off*)

HERBIE Hey, fellas. Good Luck!

YONKERS (*Brightens*) Thanks. Good luck to you, Herbie.

ANGIE Good luck, Louise.

LOUISE Good luck.

YONKERS Good luck, Madam Rose. (*Silence*) Come on, Angie.
(*They go off.* LOUISE *stands a good distance from* ROSE, *who has not moved.* HERBIE *goes to* ROSE *and speaks softly, tenderly*)

HERBIE   Rose . . . Honey, listen. I can go back in the candy business. It's steady: fifty-two weeks all year every year. I'll work my fingers to the bone; I'll do twice what I did before and that was pretty fair. Rose, I could be a district manager and we could stay put in one place. We could have our own house. Louise could go to school. Rose? Rose, honey, you still got Herbie. You can marry me and I promise you, you won't have one single worry the rest of your life. Rose, don't you want that?

LOUISE   (*A burst*)   *Yes! Momma, say yes!* (HERBIE *turns and looks at her. A moment, then she runs across the platform into his arms. He holds her tight and rocks her*) Herbie . . .

HERBIE   You read palms, I read minds. It's O.K. (*Going back to* ROSE, *brighter*) It's going to be fine now, honey. Everything happens for the best. O.K., the act's finished. But you and me and our daughter, we're going to have a home—say, we got a cow for the backyard! Why, we are going to be the best damn—

(*During the last,* ROSE *slowly gets up and brushes* HERBIE *aside as though she has not heard a word. The letter hangs from her hand as she walks—as though in a trance—to* LOUISE. *Her voice is flat and deadly calm*)

ROSE   I'm used to people walking out. When my own mother did it, I cried for a week. Your father did it, and then the man I married after him did it, and now—(*Unaware, she tears the letter in half*) Well this time, I'm not crying. This time, I'm apologizing. To you. I pushed you aside for her. I made everything only for her.

LOUISE   No, Momma.

ROSE   (*Looks at the torn letter*)   But she says I can't make her an actress like she wants to be. (*Puts torn letter in her dress. Her voice gets stronger, takes on color*) The boys walk because they think the act's finished. They think we're nothing without her. (*Now beginning to build in volume and strength and passion*) Well, she's nothing without me! I'm her mother and I made her! And I can make you now! And I will, my baby, I swear I will! I'm going to *make* you a star! (*She is carried away now by her own determination and emotion that she does not see the look that has come over* LOUISE's *face. With enthusiasm—*)I'm going to build a whole new act—all around you! It's going to be better than anything we ever did before! Better than anything we even dreamed!

HERBIE   Rose!

ROSE   (*Like a gallant, joyous express train*)   You're right, Herbie! It *is* for the best! The old act was getting stale and tired! But the new one?! Look at the new star, Herbie! She's going to be beautiful! She *is* beautiful! Finished?! We're just beginning and there's no stopping us this time! (*Her face alive with fight and plans and happiness, she roars into a violently joyous song about how great everything is going to be*)
I had a dream,
A dream about you, Baby!
It's gonna come true, Baby!
They think that we're through,
But,
Baby,

You'll be swell, you'll be great,
Gonna have the whole world on a plate!
Starting here, starting now,
   Honey, everything's coming up roses!
Clear the decks, clear the tracks,
You got nothing to do but relax!
Blow a kiss, take a bow—
   Honey, everything's coming up roses!
Now's your inning—
   Stand the world on its ear!
Set it spinning,
'N that'll be just the beginning!
Curtain up, light the lights,
You got nothing to hit but the heights!
You'll be swell,
   You'll be great,
I can tell—
   Just you wait!
That lucky star I talk about is due!
Honey, everything's coming up roses for me and for you!

You can do it,
   All you need is a hand.
We can do it,
Momma is gonna see to it!
Curtain up, light the lights,
We got nothing to hit but the heights!
I can tell,
   Wait and see!
There's the bell,
   Follow me,

And nothing's gonna stop us till we're through!
Honey, everything's coming up roses and daffodils,
Everything's coming up sunshine and Santa Claus,
Everything's gonna be bright lights and lollipops,
Everything's coming up roses for me and for you!

>(HERBIE *and* LOUISE *stand silent, numb, as she plows on,*
singing triumphantly)

The Curtain Falls

ACT TWO

Scene One

Before the curtain, the illuminated placards read:

MME. ROSE'S TOREADORABLES

TEXAS

It is desert country. Late afternoon. The rear end of a touring car sticks out from one side. From the other, part of a tent.

ROSE (*Calling*) Are you ready, Louise?

LOUISE (*Off*) Yes, Momma.

ROSE Ready, girls?

GIRLS (*Off*) Yes, Madam Rose.

ROSE Now don't let the past discourage you. Remember: you're artists of the theatre! (*She imitates a trumpet call*) Madam Rose's Toreadorables!
    (*A crash of Spanish-type music and an assortment of* GIRLS *lurches on in ghastly, homemade señorita costumes. What they lack in talent—everything—they make up for in enthusiasm. And what do they sing? The same opening as the* NEWSBOYS *and* FARMBOYS, *their predecessors*)

GIRLS (*As* ROSE *yells for them to "Sing out!"*)
    Extra! Extra! Hey, look at the headline!

83

Historical news is being made!
Extra! Extra! They're drawing a red line
Around the biggest scoop of the decade!
A barrel of charm, a fabulous thrill!
The biggest little headline in vaud-e-ville!

ROSE   Now sell it! Sell it! And give it atmosphere!

GIRLS   Presenting—in person—that five-foot-four bundle of dy-
namite: SEÑORITA LOUISE!

ROSE   Come on, Louise, come on!
(LOUISE *comes on in a glittering, gaudy toreador costume
—and a blond wig. She makes a pathetic attempt to twirl
and do a split like* JUNE *before saying—*)

LOUISE   Olé, everybody! My name's Louise. What's yours?
(*She looks up at* ROSE *in appeal. A pause. Then—*)

ROSE   Well—it's coming along.

LOUISE   Momma, I'm just no good at it.

ROSE   Don't be silly. Let's try the finale. After all, if you have a
good strong finish, they'll forgive anything! (*The* cow *runs
on*) You're late . . . Now, girls, make it stirring! (*She again
imitates a trumpet call—and the music launches into—surprise
—"The Stars and Stripes."* LOUISE *tries vainly to twirl that
same baton*) Pick your feet up, Louise, pick 'em up! (HERBIE
strolls on wearily in time for the finale: the GIRLS *remove their
Spanish shawls and turn them around to form an American
flag. But the stars are on bottom, there is much switching and*

84

when the last note is ended, the stars are in place but some of the stripes go the wrong way. ROSE *looks at* HERBIE's *face*) I guess they're tired. Up to your tent, girls. Get ready for bed.

AGNES (*One of the girls*)   Good night, Madam Rose.

ROSE   Good night, Louise. (ROSE *takes the blond wig from* LOUISE *and kisses her good night. Then she calls to the others*) Don't forget to write your mothers. For money! (*To* HERBIE) How'd you make out in town?

HERBIE   Not even a lodge hall.

ROSE   They're too damn un-American down here, that's the trouble. (*Starts to brush the wig*) We better talk about heading up north after I tell the girls their bedtime story.

HERBIE   Once upon a time, there was a prince named Ziegfeld—

ROSE   It could happen!. . . Anyway, everybody needs something impossible to hope for.

HERBIE   Rose . . . Why do you make Louise wear that wig in the act?

ROSE   It makes her look more like—a star.

HERBIE   And why do you keep that cow?

ROSE   Herbie, if that cow goes, I go! (*As* LOUISE *enters behind them in pajamas*) The act can be fixed. If I was doing it for June, I'd have it all set.

LOUISE But you're not, and I'm not June.

HERBIE Now, Plug, nobody expects you to—

LOUISE (*Quietly*) Herbie, I love you very much but you always let everything slide.

ROSE He does not!

LOUISE (*Quietly*) Momma, I love you so much I've tried hard as I could. The act is rotten and I'm rotten in it.

ROSE How do you like that? Typical of a kid!

LOUISE I've been wanting to say this—

ROSE Always impatient!

LOUISE Momma—

ROSE A few break-in dates don't go too hot so she—

LOUISE (*Grabs the wig out of* ROSE's *hand and throws it away*) Momma, I am not June! I am not a blonde! I can't do what she did!

HERBIE She's not asking you to.

LOUISE Maybe you want to stay in show business—

ROSE Maybe??

LOUISE Well, I thought—

ROSE   That's our whole life! What've we been working for ever
since you were a baby? . . . Maybe I've been on the wrong
track with you and the material, but like the good Lord says,
you gotta take the rough with the smooth, Baby. And like I
always said, you're lucky—because you don't have to take it
alone. Right, Herbie?

HERBIE   Right.

ROSE   You got Herbie for brains; we got you for talent; and you
both got me—to yell at. (*She sings*)
Wherever we go,
Whatever we do,

We're gonna go through it together.
We may not go far.
But sure as a star,
Wherever we are, it's together!

Wherever I go, I know he goes.
Wherever I go, I know she goes.
No fits, no fights, no feuds and no egos—
Amigos, together!

Through thick and through thin,
All out or all in,
And whether it's win, place or show,
With you for me and me for you
We'll muddle through whatever we do
Together, wherever we go!

87

(ROSE *holds out her hands to them. They start to sway together*)

ALL

Wherever we go,
Whatever we do,
We're gonna go through it together.

ROSE

Wherever we sleep—

LOUISE

If prices are steep—

HERBIE

We'll always sleep cheaper together.

ROSE

Whatever the boat I row, you row—

HERBIE

A duo!

ROSE

Whatever the row I hoe, you hoe—

LOUISE

A trio!

ROSE

And any IOU I owe, you owe—

HERBIE
Who, me? Oh,
No, you owe!

LOUISE
No, we owe—

ALL
Together!
We all take the bow,

ROSE
Including the cow,

ALL
Though business is lousy and slow.

ROSE
With Herbie's vim, Louise's verve—

HERBIE *and* LOUISE
Now all we need is someone with nerve—

ROSE (*Giving them a look*)
Together—

HERBIE *and* LOUISE
Together—

ROSE
Wherever—

HERBIE *and* LOUISE
Wherever—

ALL
Together wherever we go!

ROSE
If I start to dance,

HERBIE *and* LOUISE
We both start to dance,

ALL
And sometimes by chance we're together.

ROSE
If I sing B flat—ohhhh—

LOUISE
We both sing B flat—ohhhh—

HERBIE
We all can be flat—ohhhh—

ALL
Together!

HERBIE (*Twirling a pie plate*)
Whatever the trick, we can do it!

LOUISE (*Twirling a pie plate*)
With teamwork we're bound to get through it!

ROSE (*Twirling a third pie plate*)
　　There really isn't anything to it—
　　You do it.
　　　　(*They toss the plates in the air as if to catch them—the
　　　　trick is a disaster*)
　　I knew it—

ALL
　　We blew it—
　　Together!
　　We go in a group,
　　We tour in a troupe,
　　We land in the soup
　　But we know:
　　The things we do, we do by threes,
　　A perfect team—
　　　　(LOUISE *heads off in the wrong direction*)

ROSE
　　No, this way, Louise!
　　Together—

HERBIE *and* LOUISE
　　Wherever—

ALL
　　Together wherever we go!
　　　　(AGNES *enters with letters*)

AGNES   Here are the letters, Madam Rose.

ROSE   That's a good girl. Now go to bed, Agnes.

AGNES   Now that I'm an actress, it's Amanda.

ROSE   Whatever it is, go to bed.

AGNES   Could I please ask Herbie a question first?

HERBIE   Sure.

AGNES   Herbie . . . do you think we'll ever work again?

ROSE   Of course we will!

HERBIE   I'll get us a booking, Amanda.

AGNES   Thank you, Herbert. (*Turns to go, then sees the wig*) Oh, Louise, your hair!

LOUISE   It's yours if you want it.

AGNES   Gee, I always wanted to be a blonde!

ROSE (*Taking the wig from her*)   Then get some peroxide and a toothbrush. Wigs are expensive. (AGNES *goes off*. ROSE *looks at the wig*) You know, we could get a nice refund on this—if we'd ever paid for it.

HERBIE   How about getting a gallon of peroxide and a carton of toothbrushes?

ROSE What for?

HERBIE Make 'em all blondes!

ROSE I was only joking, Herbie.

HERBIE So was I, honey.

LOUISE But why not do it?

ROSE They're children, Louise!

LOUISE They're young girls, **Momma**. With blond hair, they could be pretty young girls.

HERBIE With a stretch of imagination, they might be. It'd sure jazz up the act and make it easier to sell. We could call it, Madam Rose's Blond Babies.

ROSE Baby Blondes!

LOUISE Nothing with babies.

HERBIE Hollywood Blondes.

LOUISE Yes!

ROSE All blondes except you—because you're the star!

LOUISE If I'm the star, it should be: *Louise* and Her Hollywood Blondes.

93

ROSE (*Looks at her—then*)   *Rose* Louise and Her Hollywood Blondes.

LOUISE   O.K.

ALL (*Singing*)
Through thick and through thin,
All out or all in
And whether it's win, place or show,
With you for me and me for you
We'll muddle through whatever we do
Together, wherever we go!

The Lights Dim Out

SCENE TWO

The placards change to read:

"THE BOTTOM"
WICHITA

Backstage. At one side, there is a large theatre dressing room. A long corridor leads to the "stage" (presumably on the opposite side, offstage). The corridor continues (unseen) behind the dressing room, thus leading to other, unseen dressing rooms. A large door opens into the theatre alley.

During the scene, snatches of brassy music come from the "stage." Right now, there is silence as the alley door opens and AGNES *and three or four other* GIRLS *in the act come in. Each is awed; each carries bags, props, part of the cow; and each has hair of the same, exact hideous shrieking shade of white blond.*

AGNES (*In happy awe*)   It's a real live theatre!

MAN'S VOICE (*Off*)   Let in the traveler!

MARJORIE MAY (*Looking off*)   With a real live stage! Don't you love it?

AGNES   Oh, Marjorie May, we've arrived at last!
(*They squeal and hug each other as* LOUISE—*in slacks— enters from the alley, also carrying bags, props and the* COW's *head*)

DOLORES   Louise, look!

95

AGNES   A real live theatre!

MAN *(Off)*   Will you kill them floods?

LOUISE *(Happily)*   It's just like opening day rehearsals used to be! Oh, Momma's going to love it!

MAN *(Off)*   Will you kill them floods?

PASTEY *(Off)*   Will you shut your hole?

AGNES *(Shocked)*   She isn't going to love that!

MARJORIE MAY *(Pointing to the "stage")*   Or *that!*

AGNES   What kind of a act is that?

PASTEY *(Off)*   O.K., jailbait! *(He enters: a young snot, with clipboard and pencil)* You the Hollywood Blondes?

LOUISE   Yes. I'm—

PASTEY   You're late.

LOUISE   Well, our car broke down and—

PASTEY   Skip it. Some of you dogs can use this dressing room, and the rest of you the one past it. The first one you share with Tessie Tura, the Texas Twirler—

LOUISE   My mother doesn't—

PASTEY The second with Mazeppa, Revolution in Dance. Shake it up. (*Starts to go, then turns back*) So you're the act that's supposed to keep the cops out. Boy, you must be lousy!
  (*He exits. A moment of deflation. Then—*)

LOUISE It's a real live theatre, all right.

AGNES He reminds me of my brother.

LOUISE Don't start sniveling, Amanda. Take the cow and anything else you can carry in there. Marjorie May, you take the other girls into the second room and start unpacking.
  (*She starts with props and bags for the big dressing room. The others pick up their stuff and start after her. Thus, all their backs are turned and they do not see two girls who enter from the "stage" to get a gilded spear from a stack leaning against the corridor wall. Each of these bored females wears a gladiator helmet, gladiator boots and carries a large shield in front of her. As they return to the "stage," we see that the shield is the only thing that covers them. They are nude. In the dressing room, LOUISE and AGNES have started to hang up costumes*)

AGNES Oooh, look at this! (*She is holding up a jeweled G-string, which she proceeds to try on as a necklace*) That Tessie Tura must be a very fancy lady!

LOUISE (*Trying to clean a messy dressing table*) She must also be a pig!
  (*ROSE enters through the alley door, carrying more bags and props*)

ROSE Louise?

LOUISE In here, Momma. (*Goes to the door*) Let me help you.

ROSE (*Looking around*) Baby, we're back in a theatre! We're back in a real theatre!

LOUISE Momma, where's Herbie?

ROSE He went around front to check our billing. Louise, I need you here to help me with the rest of the things. (*To the* STAGE-HAND, *who crosses*) Good morning!
(*As she turns back, she stops dead and her mouth drops open.* LOUISE *turns and she gapes too. One hand on the curtain at the edge of the "stage," throwing wild bumps savagely, is* TESSIE TURA, *a blowsy stripper wearing almost nothing besides a G-string, which does not bump with her. She looks up, during her exercises*)

TESSIE It ain't weighted right, goddamit. (MAZEPPA—*a pseudo-exotic grand stripper dressed as Queen of the Gladiators—writhes past* TESSIE *to get her spear from the wall*) It scratches hell outa me and it just don't bump when I do.

MAZEPPA Maybe there's something wrong with your bumper.
(*She exits*)

TESSIE Big joke. (*To* ROSE) I'm out there bumpin' my brains off with no action and she's bein' witty! (*To* AGNES, *who is gaping at her from the dressing-room doorway*) Hey you with the neck! I paid six bucks for that G-string. Back where you found it!

AGNES Yes, ma'am.
> (*She curtsies and scurries back in as* TESSIE *goes off.* ROSE *looks at* LOUISE)

ROSE (*Low*) Get the bags. Get the cow. Get the props.

LOUISE Now, Momma—

ROSE You don't know what kind of people are out there on that stage. You don't know what kind of a theatre this is.

LOUISE Yes I do. It's a house of burlesque.

ROSE A house of burlesque. Do you know what that is? Filth, that's what! I tell you, when your friend Herbie shows his face—

LOUISE Momma, I'm sure Herbie didn't know—

ROSE (*Picking up the props, etc., which keep dropping*) Not much, he didn't know! Agnes!

LOUISE He got the booking over the telephone—

ROSE Agnes!

LOUISE We were all so happy—

ROSE (*Storming to the dressing-room door*) AGNES, DAM-
MIT!

AGNES Madam Rose, you know my name is—

ROSE Your name is Agnes and I want you and the other girls
out of this hell hole in two seconds flat.

AGNES But, Madam—

ROSE March!

AGNES Yes, ma'am.
(*She comes out.* ROSE *goes inside and starts to pack up
what has been unpacked*)

LOUISE (*To* AGNES) Wait in the other room.
(AGNES *disappears behind the dressing room as* LOUISE
goes in)

ROSE You take the rear end of the cow, I'll take the front and
what bags we can't carry, your friend Herbie can damn well
pick up and carry himself. (LOUISE *shuts the door.* ROSE *turns
and looks at* LOUISE *leaning against it. Her voice is low and
cold*) Now you listen to me, Louise. Just because you think
your friend Herbie can do no wrong—

LOUISE This has nothing to do with Herbie.

ROSE You don't know what burlesque is.

LOUISE Yes I—

ROSE NO YOU DON'T. No daughter of mine is going to work in burlesque. And no daughter of any woman I know—

LOUISE Then where *are* we going to work?

ROSE I'd rather starve!

LOUISE Momma, how much money do we have? Including what's left of their allowances, how much money do we have?

ROSE Something'll turn up.

LOUISE It *has* turned up and *this is it!* We're flat broke, Momma. We've *got* to take this job . . . Even if you wanted to quit and go home, we'd have to take it.
(ROSE *stops in the act of taking a costume off a hook. A pause. Then abruptly, heavily, she sits*)

ROSE I had a dream . . .

LOUISE Momma . . .

ROSE You'll like this one. I had it over a week ago, only I didn't want to tell. I was home in Seattle, and the cow came into my room. But she wasn't dancing and smiling this time. She was wheezing and sad-like. She came over to the bed and looked at me and she said: "Rose, move over."

LOUISE I'm sorry, Momma.

ROSE (*Smiles*) Why? She didn't ask you to move over.

LOUISE I mean I'm sorry I'm not good enough. In the act.

ROSE Oh, it's the act that ain't good enough, Baby. Or something.
(HERBIE *hurries in through the alley door*)

HERBIE Rose?

LOUISE (*Opens the dressing-room door*) In here, Herbie.

HERBIE (*Runs in*) Rose, I didn't know, believe me.

ROSE I do, honey. What the hell! The money's good, it's only
two weeks, and maybe by that time, something'll turn up.
Right?

LOUISE Right.

HERBIE You're a nice girl, Rose. Thank you.

ROSE Well—that's show business.
(*She starts to unpack again*)

LOUISE One good thing: I'll bet we got top billing.

HERBIE Well—actually, they kind of had us lost in the middle.
I thought last was better, so it says: "*And* Rose Louise and
Her Hollywood Blondes." And I'm making them put a box
around it.

ROSE Forget the box, Herbie.

LOUISE But, Momma, if—

ROSE You don't know what they say in the business. But Herbie does. They say when a vaudeville act plays in burlesque, that means it's all washed up. (*Pause*) Herbie . . . nothin's gonna turn up for us, is it?

HERBIE No.

ROSE I guess it is a pretty rotten act.

HERBIE It ain't the act, honey. I been telling you, vaudeville's dead . . . stone cold dead.

ROSE Well—we sure as hell tried!

HERBIE You sure as hell did. Right?

LOUISE Right.

HERBIE Well, I better get the cues ready.
      (*He goes to the door*)

ROSE Herbie—how about marrying me?

HERBIE (*Turns around. A moment. Then, casually*) Sure!

ROSE I love you, you know.

HERBIE I know.

LOUISE   Do it today!

ROSE   Not while we're in burlesque!

HERBIE   The day we close.

ROSE   It's a deal. (*They shake hands and suddenly kiss*) I do, Herbie, I do.

HERBIE   So do I, Rose.
(PASTEY *barges in. During the following,* TESSIE *appears in the corridor*)

PASTEY   Hey, Rose Louise, where the hell's your music and light cues?

HERBIE   I'll be right with you.

PASTEY (*Snotty*)   You Rose Louise?

HERBIE   Yeah, I'm Rose Louise.

PASTEY   Things're looking up. Well, I got a show to open, Rose Louise, so move your ass.
(*Before* PASTEY *can get out,* HERBIE *has grabbed him, whirled him around and cracked him in the face. Then, holding him by the scruff of his neck—*)

HERBIE   Listen, you little punk. For the next two weeks, you're gonna speak like a Sunday School teacher. You have something in this theatre you probably never saw before. A lady.

(Points him toward ROSE*)* Look at her. That is a lady. *(Points him toward* LOUISE*)* That is also a lady. Every girl in this damn act is a lady, you understand?

PASTEY   Yes, sir.

HERBIE   Now get on stage and I'll give you those cues when I'm ready.

PASTEY   Yes, sir. Excuse me, ma'am.
       (He goes out and off. ROSE *kisses* HERBIE. *He goes out but is stopped in the corridor by* TESSIE*)*

TESSIE   Oh, sir? Won't you give *me* your protection? I'm a lady, too! *(On the last, a vivacious grind and bump. The bumper flips)* Hey! The goddam thing worked! *(She goes into the dressing room as* HERBIE *goes off to the "stage")* If you ladies will excuse me—

ROSE   We're very busy.

TESSIE   In *my* dressing room.

ROSE   In *your* dress—

LOUISE *(Overlapping)*   Momma—

TESSIE   You're damn right. And I don't like sharing it any more than you do. Particularly with a troupe of professional virgins.

ROSE   We are not—

TESSIE   All right, so you're acrobats.

ROSE   We happen to be headliners from the Orpheum Circuit. We were booked into this theatre by mistake.

TESSIE   Weren't we all! (*Reaching for a costume* ROSE *has unpacked*) Say! Who made that?

LOUISE   I did. I make all our costumes.

TESSIE   My! Look at them ladylike little stitches! That miserable broad who makes my gowns must be usin' a fish hook!

LOUISE   What do you pay her?

TESSIE   Twenty-five bucks a gown and I provide the material.

ROSE   Thirty.

TESSIE   She's new in the business!

ROSE   Thirty.

TESSIE   Who're you? Her mother?

ROSE   Yes.

TESSIE   Thirty. I'll get the material after the matinée.

ROSE   It's a deal. (*To* LOUISE) Where's your toreador costume?

LOUISE The girls must have it in the dressing room with them.

ROSE God knows what else they've got in there with them! (*She exits*)

TESSIE You know, from the way that dame walks, she would have made a damn good stripper in her day.
(*A burly man,* CIGAR, *the manager enters*)

CIGAR Hey, Tessie, I'm short a talking woman.

TESSIE Tough titty.

CIGAR The new comic won't use a chorus girl.

TESSIE Then let him use Mazeppa. (*To* LOUISE) Everyone else has.
(*She laughs at her joke*)

CIGAR Now you know Mazeppa's got her Gladiator Ballet just before his spot.

TESSIE Cut the ballet. It stinks anyway.

CIGAR Be a sport. I'm in a bind.

TESSIE You're always in a bind in this flea-bitten trap. I'm a strip woman, slob. I don't do no scenes. Now screw! (*To* LOUISE) You ever hear of a strip woman playing scenes? Well, you play stock in a dump like this, you gotta expect to be insulted.

CIGAR The work is steady, ain't it?

TESSIE But you bring in a new star for each show, don't you?

CIGAR Tessie, it's just a few lines—

TESSIE Fat boy, save your bad breath.

CIGAR I'll give you ten bucks extra.

TESSIE Nah.

LOUISE (*As* ROSE *returns*) I can read lines.

CIGAR Who're you?

LOUISE Rose Louise. Of Rose Louise and Her Hollywood Blondes.

ROSE Wait a minute. What kind of lines?

CIGAR You in her act?

ROSE Well, not exactly.

CIGAR Shut up. (*To* LOUISE) How are your legs?

TESSIE Great! And I'll learn her the scenes.

CIGAR O.K. Ten bucks.
       (*He goes*)

LOUISE   It's money, Momma.

ROSE (*Going to* TESSIE)   What is she going to be saying out there on that stage?

TESSIE   The same burlesque junk that's been said since the Year One. Say, where you been all your life?

ROSE (*Proudly*)   Playing vaudeville.

TESSIE   Where? In the Vatican?

ROSE   You name a big city and we've played it!

LOUISE   My grandpa says we've covered the country like Gypsies!

TESSIE   Yeah? Well, you may be a Gypsy, Rose Louise—say, that ain't a bad name if you ever take up stripping—

ROSE   She won't!

TESSIE   No! But you'll let her feed lines to a bum comic for a lousy ten bucks a week!

ROSE   That's training: she's going to be an actress! This is only temporary! After we finish here, she goes right back to vaudeville!
       (*She turns away—and sees* LOUISE's *look. Embarrassed, she sits*)

TESSIE (*Quietly*) Back to vaudeville, my eye. There ain't any vaudeville left except burlesque.

LOUISE We know.

TESSIE *You* know. You better wise *her* up.

LOUISE (*Sudden burst*) She's wise! (*Holding* ROSE) She's a damn sight wiser than any of you!

TESSIE (*Shrugs*) Like mother, like daughter. O.K. (ROSE *exits with the makeup kit and heads for the other dressing room.* TESSIE *turns to* LOUISE, *perplexed*) Say, whose feelings did I hurt? Yours or hers?

LOUISE (*Smiles*) Neither. We'll both be fine.

TESSIE I hope so, because sharing a dressing room is like sleeping together. And if you don't get along with—
       (MAZEPPA *comes storming in with* ELECTRA, *another stripper*)

MAZEPPA Miss Tura, I'll thank you not to give the boss any notion that I would ever play scenes. And one more disparaging remark about my ballet will find this bugle right up your—

TESSIE Please: there's a lady present!

MAZEPPA Where?

TESSIE Open your eyes instead of your mouth.

TESSIE Gypsy, meet Miss Mazeppa—and Miss Electra.

ELECTRA Say, you're even younger than I was when I began stripping.

LOUISE I'm not going to strip.

MAZEPPA (*Belligerent*) Something wrong with stripping?

LOUISE No. I just meant I don't have any talent.

TESSIE You think they have? I myself of course was a ballerina. But take it from me, to be a stripper all you need to have is no talent.

MAZEPPA You'll pardon me, but to have no talent is not enough. What you need is an idea that makes your strip special.
>   (*During the following number, each of the three strippers demonstrates the gimmick that has made her a "star."*
>   MAZEPPA *sings*)
You can pull all the stops out
Till they call the cops out,
Grind your behind till you're banned,
But you gotta get a gimmick
If you wanna get a hand.

You can sacrifice your sacro
Workin' in the back row,
Bump in a dump till you're dead.
Kid, you gotta get a gimmick
If you wanna get ahead.

You can—!, you can—!, you can—!!!
That's how burlesque was born.
So I—! and I—! and I—!!!
But I do it with a horn!

> (*She demonstrates: bumping and grinding like mad while she blows army calls on her bugle*)

Once I was a schlepper,
Now I'm Miss Mazeppa
With my Revolution in Dance.
You gotta have a gimmick
If you wanna have a chance!!

ELECTRA (*Singing*)

She can—!, she can—!, she can—!!!
They'll never make her rich.
Me, I—! and I—! and I—!!!
But I do it with a switch!

> (*She demonstrates: punctuating* her *bumps and grinds with electric lights which illuminate her strategic points*)

I'm electrifying,
And I'm not even trying.
I never have to sweat to get paid.
'Cause if you got a gimmick,
Gypsy girl, you've got it made.

TESSIE (*Singing*)

All them—!s and them—!s and them—!!!s
Ain't gonna spell success.

Chotzi Foley, Maria Karnilova, and Faith
Dane, as ELECTRA, TESSIE TURA, and MAZEPPA

Me, I—! and! I—! and I—!!!
But I do it with finesse!
  (*And she demonstrates: a broken-down version of ballet
  climaxed with the same eternal bumps and grinds*)
Dressy Tessie Tura
Is so much demurer
Than all them other ladies because
You gotta get a gimmick
If you wanna get applause!

ALL

Do somethin' special;
Anything that's fresh'll
Earn you a big fat cigar.
You're more than just a mimic
When you got a gimmick—
Take a look how different we are!
  (*They bump and grind: what else?*)

ELECTRA

If you wanna make it,
Shake it till you break it.

TESSIE

If you wanna grind it,
Wait till you've refined it.

MAZEPPA

If you wanna bump it,
Bump it with a trumpet!

ALL

Get yourself a gimmick
And you too
Can be a star!

The Lights Black Out

Scene Three

The scene is the backstage corridor.

STAGEHAND (*To* PASTEY, *who is crossing*) Kill the floods and bring in number four!

PASTEY I tole ya we ain't usin' number four this show, ya pinhead!

HERBIE (*Runs on with a little bouquet*) Hey, you seen Amanda?

PASTEY She must be packin'. Ain't your act through today?

HERBIE (*Joyously*) You bet it is! Through—finished—over!
(AGNES *comes on with a suitcase.* HERBIE *crosses to her*)

PASTEY (*To the* STAGEHAND) Will you kill number four?
(*He exits*)

HERBIE (*To* AGNES) I've been hunting for you. Here.
(*He gives her the bouquet*)

AGNES Oh, Herbie, it's like for a funeral!

HERBIE It's for the wedding! Madam Rose and I want you to be bridesmaid, Amanda.

AGNES It's Agnes again.

HERBIE (*Hugs her*) You'll be happier as Agnes, Amanda. (*Dashing off*) See you out front.

TESSIE (*Runs on*) Oh, you're leaving and I didn't get you a momento!

AGNES My career as an actress is over. I have to go home and let my hair grow out.

TESSIE Ya poor kid.

PASTEY (*Off*) Tessie!

TESSIE Well—for the last time: (*Doing a grind*) Meet ya round the corner (AGNES *joins in*) in a half-hour.
   (AGNES *breaks down on* TESSIE's *bosom*)

PASTEY TESSIE!

TESSIE TESSIE! I'm coming, ya creep!
   (*She hurries to the wings leading to the "stage." A farewell wave to* AGNES, *a lift to her sagging bosoms—and she floats off like a ballerina*)

The Lights Black Out

Scene Four

The dressing room looks emptier. Most of ROSE's *belongings have been packed.*

The lights are different. The corridor is darker but streaked with colored light coming from the "stage," where the show is on: a production number, to judge from the music which is continuous under the scene. HERBIE—*in a different suit*—ROSE *and* LOUISE—*in coats*—*are finishing packing.* ROSE *is very subdued;* HERBIE *is very up;* LOUISE *keeps watching* ROSE.

HERBIE (*To* ROSE) Why aren't you nervous? I've never been so nervous in my whole life!

LOUISE (*Hands* ROSE *a baton*) You've never been married before.

HERBIE Well, your mother's never been married like she's going to be this time. For keeps and forever—to me! Ain't you a *little* nervous, honey!

ROSE Sure.

LOUISE She's a little sad, too. About the girls.

HERBIE (*Admiring the marriage license*) Say, the minister doesn't keep this, does he? I want to have it framed. Framed and hanging in our living room.

LOUISE (*Holding the* cow *head*) What about this, Momma?

ROSE Take it.

HERBIE Rose—

LOUISE (*Putting the* COW *head on the suitcase*) We can hang her up in the living room, too, Herbie. Over the mantelpiece.

HERBIE Rose honey, it ain't that I don't know what you're feeling. Or that I don't know I oughta shut up. But I'm so goddam happy, I can't! (CIGAR *and* PASTEY *enter the corridor from the "stage." Their dialogue and* HERBIE'S *are simultaneous.* ROSE *listens to* HERBIE) I'm finally getting everything I wanted! Even a fancy ceremony with bridesmaids. Of course, what the minister's going to say when he gets a load of all that hair, I don't know. But the hell with him! (ROSE's *attention shifts to the hall*) All he's gotta say is, Do you, Rose, take him, Herbie?

CIGAR I don't know why the hell I stay in this business. If it ain't one damn headache, it's another!

PASTEY Ssh! They'll hear you out front.

CIGAR It's my theatre, ain't it? Let 'em! Last show, no talking woman. Show before that, no second banana. If that crazy broad wasn't here, why did you start the performance?

PASTEY She don't go on till next to closing, and she said she was only goin' next door to the drugstore.
        (HERBIE *and then* LOUISE *become aware that* ROSE *is standing dead still, listening. They stand, watching her, tense, afraid*)

CIGAR What'd they arrest her for? Shoplifting?

PASTEY No, soliciting.

CIGAR She always was greedy. Well, cut the spot.

HERBIE Honey, do you think we can invite the minister for a drink after?

PASTEY It's the star strip!

CIGAR Cut it.

PASTEY They'll yell murder if it's only the same bags they've been seeing the last eight weeks. The star's the novelty!

CIGAR Whaddya want me to do? Let you strip?
(ROSE *throws down whatever she is holding and walks swiftly out of the dressing room into the corridor*)

ROSE My daughter can do it. (*They look at her. She steps back, as though afraid of herself*) Rose Louise.

PASTEY Since when?

ROSE Since she's been here to see how little there is to it.

CIGAR She didn't look bad in them scenes.

ROSE She'll look great in her own gowns.

PASTEY What's the gimmick?

CIGAR She's young. And you got any better ideas?

PASTEY (*As he exits*) Well, she better get ready right damn now.

ROSE It's the star spot.

CIGAR You telling me?

ROSE That means the star salary.

CIGAR If we keep her.

ROSE You will. She's going to be wonderful! (CIGAR *goes off as* ROSE *runs excitedly into the dressing room and begins opening a suitcase.* HERBIE *and* LOUISE *stand dead still, watching*) I knew something would turn up! Where's that dress you were gonna make for Tessie? It'll work perfect for you! . . . (*Gets the dress out*) Well, get your makeup on, there ain't much time! . . . Oh, silly, you're not really gonna strip! All you'll do is walk around the stage in time to the music and drop a shoulder strap at the end. (*Takes out the makeup*) You're a lady—like Herbie says you are! You just parade so grand they'll think it's a favor if you even show them your knee— Louise, it's the star spot! I promised my daughter we'd be a star! (*Still,* LOUISE *just stands.* ROSE *speaks quietly now*) Baby, it's all right to walk out when they *want* you. But you can't walk out when after all these rotten years, we're still a flop. That's quitting. (*A brief burst*) We can't quit because we're a flop! Louise . . . don't be like June. Just do this, and then we can walk away proud because we made it! Maybe only in burlesque, maybe only in second-rate burlesque at that—but let's walk away a star! (LOUISE *unbuttons her coat.* ROSE *hugs her, helps her, then rummages for the dress as* LOUISE *begins quickly to get ready*) I guess there ain't time to finish the dress, but we can pin it easy. Hey, here's some material for extra panels! Didn't I always say you were born lucky? You can unpin the panels and drop 'em every once in a while so they'll think you're taking something off. (*Slowly,* HERBIE *folds up the license and puts it in his pocket at he walks out of the room, and disappears in the corridor.* LOUISE *is making up feverishly*) Not too much makeup, Baby. Young and girlish. Pure. Don't smear that junk all over your face like they do. You just keep your mouth the way the Lord made it . . . No rouge. No beauty marks. You be a lady: grand, elegant . . . with a classy, ladylike walk. My God! Shoes! . . . Well, we can use the old silver ones we borrowed from Tessie. (*She takes them from her own suitcase*) They'll do for this performance . . . Come on. Get into 'em. (*As* LOUISE *does*) Oh, no—your hair's wrong. You can't let it just hang like spaghetti. Put it up! Like Momma's! It's got to have class! Puff it out in front. Thank God, the Lord gave us good color—and that you washed it this morning . . . Say, do you think we should put a couple of feathers in? (*Tries some*) No, that's what they all do. (*Tosses them aside*) Jewelry? No. Let Tessie and the others wear all the vulgar junk they want.

PASTEY (*Rushes in*)   She almost ready? She goes on in five minutes.

ROSE (*Pushing him out*)   She'll be there—she'll be there! Come on, get into the dress. (LOUISE *exits through another door, presumably leading into a bathroom, to change into the strip dress.* ROSE *picks up a pair of long white gloves*) Whose are these? Oh—my wedding present from Tessie. Good for a lady. Wear 'em . . . Now, what else? . . . Music! (*Flips*

through sheet music in the suitcase) "Spanish"—"Cow"—
"Military"? (*Shakes her head*) No. Say, you can do June's
"Let Me Entertain You" number! I'll mark it for the conductor to repeat two choruses slow—no, two and a half choruses,
and sing out, Louise! You just walk and dip . . . you're a
lady; you make 'em beg for more—and then *don't* give it to
them! . . . Now—have I forgotten anything? Anything else?
(*On this last,* HERBIE *enters the dressing room. He is almost
shaking with anger and his effort to control it*) Where you
been? Out front?

HERBIE No, I got sick to my stomach, and threw up.

ROSE But you feel better now.

HERBIE No.

ROSE Herbie—I just had to.

HERBIE That's why I'm leaving.

ROSE I apologize.

HERBIE No, let me. For my resemblance to a mouse. No: to a
worm—the way I've crawled after you. No more, Rose. I
won't. I was even going to crawl away from you—because my
stomach started to turn over at the idea of coming back and
telling you we're finished.

ROSE Tell me tomorrow—after we're married.

HERBIE We're never getting married, Rose.

ROSE   We certainly are! First thing in the morning, we'll—

HERBIE   *Never*, Rose. Not if you went down on your knees and begged. I still love you—but all the vows from here to doomsday . . . they couldn't make you a wife. I want a wife, Rose. I'm going to be a man if it kills me.

ROSE   (*Angrily*)   So you're killing *me!*

HERBIE   Nobody can kill you.

ROSE   You think I got a bullet-proof vest? You're jealous, that's what you are! Like every man I've ever known! Jealous—because my girls come first. Well, they always did and they always will!

HERBIE   Then why did June leave?

ROSE   I don't wanna hear her name!

HERBIE   She didn't want the act any more than Louise wants this!

ROSE   Louise does!

HERBIE   She'll leave like June did!

ROSE   Never! She's gonna be a star.

HERBIE   She's gonna be a star! If it kills *you and her*, she's gonna be a star *someplace! She's* gonna be a star. Where are *you* gonna be, Rose? Where are you gonna be when *she* gets married?

ROSE She won't be getting married for years—she's a baby!

HERBIE Sure!

ROSE Anyway, her career will always come first.
(*She sits, looks over the music defiantly*)

HERBIE That's right. That-is-right.
(*He picks up his suitcase, and starts out*)

ROSE Herbie . . . why does everybody walk out?

HERBIE Maybe Louise won't.
(*He pats her shoulder. Without looking up, she reaches for his hand and holds it there*)

ROSE Don't leave, Herbie . . . I need you.

HERBIE . . . What for?

ROSE A million things.

HERBIE Just one would be better. Good-bye, honey. (*Silence. He kisses the top of her head*) Be a good girl.
(*Quietly, he goes out the door. Music starts*)

ROSE You go to hell!
(ROSE *sits staring and* PASTEY *runs in*)

PASTEY Get her music to the conductor and you better stand by me for the light cues. I just hope you know what you're doing.
(PASTEY *races out.* ROSE *touches the place where* HERBIE kissed her)

ROSE (*Singing*)
   Lucky, you're a man who likes children—
     That's an important sign.
   Lucky, I'm a woman with children—
   Funny,
     Small and funny—
     (ROSE *gets up and slowly walks to the white gloves. She has them in her hand, and is staring at them as* LOUISE *comes out and takes the gloves from her.* ROSE *watches her start to put them on, then speaks quietly, as though dazed*)

ROSE I'll get the music to the conductor. Just remember—you're a lady. (*With anguished determination*) And you-are-going-to-be-a-star!
     (*Music in hand, she walks out, leaving* LOUISE *alone before a long mirror in the dressing room. As she draws on the white gloves, the music ends and the light in the corridor goes very dark. There is a soft glow on the mirror as dark figures scurry through the corridor outside saying: "Let's watch from the wings." "No, I'm going out front." "What's she gonna do?" "She isn't the type." "She'll quit halfway through." "How do you know?" "She'll never make it." "Come on, let's get a good place." "I'm scared for her." During this, the dressing room has been rolling off, leaving only the mirror. The only light on the stage is the glow of the mirror bulbs; the only figure is* LOUISE. *She looks at herself, goes close to the mirror to check her make-up, then suddenly stops. She touches her body lightly, moves back, straightens up and stares at her reflection. Very softly—*)

LOUISE   Momma . . . I'm pretty . . . I'm a pretty girl, Momma!
(*Very grand, very proud, very beautiful, she turns from
the mirror and begins to walk away from it, as though she
were going in the direction of the "stage." The mirror
moves off, the lights come up and we are "on the stage."
The curtain is upstage; strip music can be heard, a dim
stripper can be seen through the curtain.* ROSE, *who is
peering through, turns around and sees* LOUISE)

ROSE (*Softly*)   You look beautiful!

TESSIE (*Runs on with an old fur stole which she wraps around*
LOUISE)   For luck, honey!

ROSE   Are you nervous, Baby?

LOUISE   . . . What?

ROSE   I said, Are you nervous?

LOUISE   No, Mother.
(*The offstage music ends; there is applause as the weary
stripper comes on from behind the curtain, looks at* LOUISE
and goes off. PASTEY *grabs a microphone*)

PASTEY   Wichita's one and only Burlesque Theatre presents—

LOUISE (*Nervous after all*)   Momma—

PASTEY   Miss—Gypsy—Rose—Lee!

TESSIE (*Correcting him angrily*) Louise!
(*But he shrugs. Everyone exits but* LOUISE, *who stands alone before the curtain. A roll of the drum and lights reveal the curtain as a scrim. Through it, we can see the glow of the strippers' runway. Another drum roll: the curtains part and* LOUISE *steps forward. Another drum roll: a spotlight hits her and her head goes back as though she has been blinded. Blinding floodlights then shine directly into the eyes of the audience; then a total blackout. When the lights go on again,* LOUISE *is downstage, facing the audience before a curtain the exact replica of the one upstage. Her head is back a bit, her eyes closed, the spotlight bright on her. The small burlesque band in the pit begins "Let Me Entertain You."* LOUISE *can barely start singing.* ROSE, *from the wings, calls out*)

ROSE Sing out, Louise!
(*As* LOUISE *sings she seems to get more confidence, even to begin to enjoy herself. And her voice finally rings out true and clear. And then, unsure of exactly what to do, she begins to walk*)

CIGAR (*From the wings*) Don't just walk! Do something!

ROSE Dip! Just dip!
(LOUISE *does. After a moment*)

CIGAR Take something off!

ROSE A glove! Give 'em a glove!
(*And* LOUISE *does take off a glove. As she walks more, she begins to relax, to grow, to enjoy—until just before she*

exits, she looks at the audience humorously, and lowers one shoulder strap. The lights on the curtains change; the placards roll to read:

DETROIT

GYPSY ROSE LEE

And an ANNOUNCER'S *voice comes over the speaker*)

ANNOUNCER   The Alhambra Theatre of Detroit is happy to present that lovely newcomer, Miss Gypsy Rose Lee!

(And out she comes, in another dress, with one glove off, one shoulder strap down, as though the strip were continuous. But now she is more poised, more glinting with humor—but always, a lady. Again, the curtain lights change; again the placards roll, to read this time:

PHILADELPHIA

GYPSY ROSE LEE

And we hear an ANNOUNCER'S *voice*)

ANNOUNCER   Philadelphia's Diamond Burlesque takes pleasure in presenting that lovely new star, Miss Gypsy Rose Lee!

(The strip continues in another gown, with a big feather hat added this time. LOUISE *has grown again and no matter what she does, is, as always, the lady. And one never seen in the nude. A great drum roll; the lights on the curtains change; the placards now read:*

GYPSY ROSE LEE

MINSKY'S

And another ANNOUNCER'S *voice*)

ANNOUNCER   Minsky's World Famous Burlesque takes great pride and pleasure in presenting the Queen of the Strip Tease, the Incomparable Miss Gypsy Rose Lee—in our Salute To Xmas!

(*And the curtains open for a brief flash of a garish, loud, corny production number with nudes on a Christmas tree and slithering show girls. The* pièce de résistance *is a Christmas present brought on by comics dressed as Santa Claus. They open it—and out comes* GYPSY—*glittering like a diamond in a sewer. Her head high, she somehow has elegance as she reprises her song. At the end, she pulls the curtain across the stage with her, shutting out the production, shutting out everything but The Lady of the Strip Tease,* MISS GYPSY ROSE LEE)

The Lights Fade

The placards change to read:

"MOTHER'S DAY"
MINSKY'S

A dressing room.
The basic crumminess of the room is all but hidden by the trappings its occupant has installed: gleaming bottles; a nude statue festooned with feathers and a rhinestone G-string; souvenirs; costumes, etc.

ROSE *is hammering a spike into the wall, as she talks to* RENÉE, *the maid, who barely listens. During the following,* ROSE *hangs the* COW's *head up on the spike.*

ROSE Sure I saw that sign! If I can read the fine print in our contracts, I can certainly read letters two feet high: "THE MOTHER OF MISS GYPSY ROSE LEE IS NOT ALLOWED BACKSTAGE AT THIS THEATRE." You know what I did with that sign? (*Puts a string of beads on the* COW's *horn*) I tore it off the wall, spread it on the floor, and set Chowsie III down on it. That dog's a trouper: *she* knew what to do! . . . It'll take more than signs to keep me out of a theatre!

> (*The door opens and* LOUISE *enters in her strip costume.*
> *She is singing until she sees* ROSE. *And the* COW *head*)

LOUISE (*Angrily*) Now look, Mother—(RENÉE *quickly comes*

with a negligee and a calming look. LOUISE *points to the* COW)
Renée, that comes down.

> (*She sits at the dressing table and swiftly sets about re-
> pairing her makeup*)

ROSE   You need *something* to remind you your goal was to be a
great actress, not a cheap stripper.

LOUISE   June's the actress, Mother. And I'm not a cheap stripper. I'm the highest paid in the business.

ROSE   You won't be ready when vaudeville comes back.

LOUISE   No, I'll be dead. (*Then, indicating the furs she has
thrown on a chair*) Renée, tell Sam he can lock up the animals
for the night.

ROSE   I'll do it.

LOUISE   Mother, please. (*To* RENÉE) And bring my press agent
in as soon as he gets here.

RENÉE   O.K.
> (*She goes out with the furs and the* COW *head*)

ROSE   Since when do you fix your face before you take your
bath?

LOUISE   A photographer's coming.

ROSE   Where's he going to photograph you? In the tub?

LOUISE Eventually.

ROSE (*Shocked*) Louise!

LOUISE It's for *Vogue*.

ROSE (*Elated*) Louise!! Think I ought to freshen up?

LOUISE They only want me in the tub, Mother.
(*The telephone rings*)

ROSE I've got it.

LOUISE (*Beating* ROSE *to it*) Hello? . . . (*Intimately*) Hello.
No, it's difficult right now.

ROSE I'm not leaving.

LOUISE Let's meet at the party . . . Yes, I promise. *À bientôt*.
(*She hangs up*)

ROSE *À bien* what?

LOUISE I guess I am being a little much—but, Momma, I love it.

ROSE . . . Who's giving the party?

LOUISE Some friends.

ROSE In the old days, I was always invited first.

LOUISE   Mother—

ROSE   (*Very grandly*)   I wouldn't go even if I *did* have something to wear. I got more important things to do—like thinking up an idea for a new strip for us.

LOUISE   Mother, we're still stuck with that wind machine you bought to *blow* my clothes off . . . Actually—I'm putting in a new number on Saturday.

ROSE   . . . What is it?

LOUISE   You'll see.

ROSE   I'll see.

LOUISE   Let me surprise you.

ROSE   These days, you're just one big surprise after another . . . Well, we better go shopping tomorrow for the material for the gown.

LOUISE   I've got a French lesson tomorrow.

ROSE   Oh. Well, I'll go alone. Got any particular color in mind?

LOUISE   Mother—I've already started to make the gown.

ROSE   Oh . . . Well, I better run your bath for you.

LOUISE   You don't have to. That's what I've got a maid for.

ROSE LET ME DO SOMETHING, DAMMIT!

LOUISE (*Very quietly*) What, Mother?

ROSE A million things. I'm not a baby.

LOUISE Neither am I.

ROSE Don't you take that tone to me. Your sister used to get that edge to her voice—

LOUISE I am not June!

ROSE You're not Louise, either!

LOUISE And neither are you!

ROSE Oh, yes I am! More than you, Miss Gypsy Rose Lee—with your dirty pictures for *Vogue!*

LOUISE Mother—

ROSE And your maids and your press agents and your fancy friends with their fancy parties!

LOUISE They happen—

ROSE Your loud-mouth mother ain't invited to those goddam parties. They laugh at her!

LOUISE They don't—

ROSE THEY DO! And don't think I don't know that's one reason why you don't want me backstage: so I won't hear 'em laugh. Well, it's *them* you oughta keep out, not me! Because they're laughing at you, too! The burlesque queen who speaks lousy French and reads book reviews like they was books!

LOUISE Turn it off, Mother.

ROSE You know what you are to them? A circus freak! This year's novelty act! And when the bill is changed—

LOUISE I SAID TURN IT OFF! *Nobody laughs at me*—because I laugh first! *At* me! ME—from Seattle; me—with no education; me, with no talent—as you've kept reminding me my whole life. Look at me now: a star! Look how I live! Look at my friends! Look where I'm going! I'm not staying in burlesque. I'm moving—maybe up, maybe down—but wherever it is, I'm *enjoying* it! I'm having the time of my life because for the first time, it *is* my life! I love it! I love every second of it and I'll be damned if you're going to take it away from me! I *am* Gypsy Rose Lee! I love her—and if you don't, you can clear out *now!*
      (*A moment:* ROSE *stares at her, stunned. Then a knocking on the door and* RENÉE *enters*)

RENÉE Your press agent is here with the photographer.

LOUISE Tell him I'll be ready in a minute. (*Softly*) Momma, we can't go shouting seven performances of this a week.

ROSE The whole family shouts: it comes from our living so near the railroad tracks.

LOUISE I'm getting an ulcer.

ROSE (*She is trying to make peace*) You think I'm not?

LOUISE Yes, I think you're not. And if you want an ulcer, Momma, get one of your own. You can't have mine.

ROSE Let's forget it.

LOUISE No, let's finish it.

ROSE I should go feed Chowsie.

LOUISE Mother, you fought your whole life. I wish you could relax now—

ROSE You need more mascara on your left eye.

LOUISE *Momma, you have got to let go of me!*

ROSE Let go?

LOUISE I'll give you anything you want—

ROSE You *need* me!

LOUISE A house, a farm, a school—a dramatic school for kids? You were always great with kids!

ROSE (*Cutting in*) *I'm a pro!* Not an old work horse you can turn out to pasture just because you think you're riding high on your own!

136

LOUISE Momma, no kid does it all on his own but *I am not a kid any more!* From now on, even if I flop, I flop on my own!
(*A knock on the door*)

PHIL (*Off*) Hey, Gyps, what do you say?

ROSE "So long, Rose," that's what she says. "Don't slam the door as you leave."
(*She starts to go, but is pushed aside by the press agent and photographers who come in. She stands watching*)

PHIL (*As he enters*) Hi, Rose. Gyps, baby, may I present Monsieur Bougeron-Cochon.

LOUISE *Enchanté, monsieur.*

BOUGERON-COCHON *Enchanté.*

PHIL Let's make with the *oiseau,* kiddies. One before you take the plunge, Gyps. All set . . . (LOUISE *takes a cheesecake pose*) Fine!

ROSE All right, miss. But just one thing I want to know. All the working and pushing and fenagling . . . All the scheming and scrimping and lying awake nights figuring: how do we get from one town to the next? How do we all eat on a buck? How do I make an act out of nothing? What'd I do it for? You say I fought my whole life. I fought *your* whole life. So now tell me: *what'd I do it for?*

LOUISE (*Quietly, after a long moment*) I thought you did it for me, Momma.
(ROSE *stares. Her hands drop to her sides. She turns and quietly goes out*)

PHIL Come on, smile, Gyps. Show us your talent! (*She poses*)
That's it!
    (*The flashbulb explodes*)

The Lights Black Out

Scene Six

A lone spot picks up ROSE *as she moves down front.*

ROSE "I thought you did it for me, Momma." "I thought you did
it for me, Momma . . ." I thought you made a no-talent ox
into a star because you like doing things the hard way,
Momma. (*Louder*) And you *haven't* got any talent!—not
what *I* call talent, Miss Gypsy Rose Lee! (*The lights now begin
to come up, showing the whole stage, bare except for a few
stacked flats of scenery used earlier in the big production number.* ROSE *shouts defiantly*) I made you!—and you wanna know
why? You wanna know what I did it for?! (*Louder*) *Because
I was born too soon and started too late, that's why!* With what
I have in me, I could've been better than ANY OF YOU!
What I got in me—what I been holding down inside of me—
if I ever let it out, there wouldn't be signs big enough! There
wouldn't be lights bright enough! (*Shouting right out to
everyone now*) HERE SHE IS, BOYS! HERE SHE IS,
WORLD! HERE'S ROSE!! (*She sings*)
CURTAIN UP!!!
LIGHT THE LIGHTS!!!
    (*Speaking*)
Play it, boys.
    (*Singing*)
You either got it,
or you ain't—
And, boys, I got it!
You like it?

ORCHESTRA   Yeah!

ROSE

Well, I got it!
Some people got it
   And make it pay,
Some people can't even
   Give it away.
This people's got it
   And this people's spreadin' it around.
You either have it
   Or you've had it.
      (*Speaking*)
Hello, everybody! My name's Rose. What's yours? (*Bumps*)
How d'ya like them egg rolls, Mr. Goldstone?
      (*Singing*)
Hold your hats,
   And hallelujah,
Momma's gonna show it to ya!
      (*Speaking*)
Ready or not, here comes Momma!
      (*Singing*)
Momma's talkin' loud,
Momma's doin' fine,
Momma's gettin' hot,
Momma's goin' strong,
Momma's movin' on,
Momma's all alone,
Momma doesn't care,
Momma's lettin' loose,
Momma's got the stuff,
Momma's lettin' go—

    (*Stopping dead as the words hit her*)
Momma—
Momma's—
    (*Shaking off the mood*)
Momma's got the stuff,
Momma's got to move,
Momma's got to go—
    (*Stopping dead again, trying to recover*)
Momma—
Momma's—
Momma's gotta let go!
    (*Stops; after a moment she begins to pace*)
Why did I do it?
  What did it get me?
Scrapbooks full of me in the background.
Give 'em love and what does it get you?
What does it get you?
One quick look as each of 'em leaves you.
All your life and what does it get you?
Thanks a lot—and out with the garbage.
They take bows and you're battin' zero.
I had a dream—
I dreamed it for you,
  June,
It wasn't for me, Herbie.
And if it wasn't for me
Then where would you be,
Miss Gypsy Rose Lee!
Well, someone tell me, when is it my turn?
Don't I get a dream for myself?
Startin' now it's gonna be my turn!
Gangway, world,

Get offa my runway!
Startin' now I bat a thousand.
This time, boys, I'm takin' the bows and
Everything's coming up Rose—
Everything's coming up Roses—
Everything's coming up Roses
This time for me!
For me—
For me—
For me—
For me—
FOR ME!

> (LOUISE *comes on quietly and stands tall and beautiful in a* *mink coat over a perfect evening gown.* ROSE *turns, and* *with an embarrassed smile says—*)

Just trying out a few ideas you might want to use . . .

LOUISE (*Quietly*)   You'd really have been something, Mother.

ROSE   Think so?

LOUISE   If you had had someone to push you like I had . . .

ROSE (*Tough with herself, too, she shakes her head*)   If I could've been, I would've been. And *that's* show business . . . About that school—for kids, like you said. I could open one. Only—kids grow up. And twice is enough . . . I guess I did do it for me.

LOUISE   Why, Mother?

ROSE   Just wanted to be noticed.

LOUISE   Like I wanted you to notice me. (ROSE *turns and looks at her*) I still do, Momma. (*She holds out her arms to* ROSE, *who hesitates, then comes running to* LOUISE *like a child.* LOUISE *pats her, kisses her hair as she says*) O.K., Momma . . . O.K., Rose.

  (ROSE *clutches her, then moves away. She forces a smile as she turns back*)

ROSE   Say, you look like you should speak French!

LOUISE   You're coming to that party with me.

ROSE   No.

LOUISE   Come on.

ROSE   Like this?

LOUISE   Here. You wear my mink. I've got a stole in the box office.

ROSE   Well—just for an hour or two. Say, this looks better on me than on you! . . . Funny how we can wear the same size.

LOUISE (*A knowing look*)   Especially in mink.

ROSE   You know, I had a dream last night. (*She links her arm through* LOUISE's *as they start slowly across the stage*) It was a big poster of a mother and daughter—you know, like the cover of that ladies' magazine.

LOUISE (*Warningly*)   Yes, Mother?

ROSE (*Stops moving*)   Only it was you and me, wearing exactly the same gown. It was an ad for Minsky—and the headline said: (*She traces the name in the air*) MADAM ROSE— (LOUISE *gives her a look;* ROSE *catches it and, moving her hand up to give* LOUISE *top billing, says*) AND HER DAUGHTER, GYPSY!

(*They both begin to laugh as they walk off*)

The Curtain Falls